"If you are looking for just another collection of saccharine clichés about shiny happy Christian families, then you might want to leave this volume on the bookstore shelf. In an era when too many Christians listen more intently to television therapists than to the Bible on the question of the family, this could be one of the most significant books you ever read."

Russell D. Moore, Dean, School of Theology; Senior Vice President for Academic Administration; Professor of Theology and Ethics, The Southern Baptist Theological Seminary

"This book is a treasure trove of biblical wisdom on matters pertaining to marriage, child-rearing, singleness, and sexuality. As Western society struggles to preserve a social identity informed by Christian truths, this study reaffirms God's will for self-understanding and family ties. Readers seeking the whole counsel of God on these matters will find enormous assistance here."

Robert W. Yarbrough, Professor of New Testament, Covenant Theological Seminary

"These days it is important for us to remember that God has something to say about marriage and family. With all of the competing voices insisting on new definitions and unbiblical patterns, Köstenberger has provided the Christian community with an invaluable resource. I heartily recommend it."

Randy Stinson, Senior Fellow, Council on Biblical Manhood and Womanhood

"With the current attack on marriage and family now raging at a fevered pitch, Köstenberger's book is a vital resource that should be in the hands of every evangelical."

Tom Elliff, Pastor, First Southern Baptist Church, Del City, Oklahoma

For our precious families, with love and gratitude,
and for all who want to make our Maker's design
the blueprint for their homes and marriages

Longing to see the fulfillment of his purpose:
"to bring all things in heaven and on earth together
under one head, even Christ" (Eph 1:10 NIV)

Other Crossway Books by Andreas Köstenberger

Excellence: The Character of God and the Pursuit of Scholarly Virtue

The Heresy of Orthodoxy: How Contemporary Culture's Fascination with Diversity Has Reshaped Our Understanding of Early Christianity (with Michael J. Kruger)

God, Marriage, and Family: Rebuilding the Biblical Foundation

MARRIAGE

and the

FAMILY

Biblical Essentials

ANDREAS KÖSTENBERGER

with DAVID W. JONES

WHEATON, ILLINOIS

Library of Congress Cataloging-in-Publication Data

Köstenberger, Andreas J., 1957–
    Marriage and the family : biblical essentials / Andreas Köstenberger with David W. Jones.
        p. cm.
    Rev. ed. of: God, marriage, and family.
    Includes bibliographical references and index.
    ISBN 978-1-4335-2856-9 (tp)
    1. Marriage—Biblical teaching. 2. Families—Biblical teaching.
3. Marriage—Religious aspects—Christianity. 4. Families—Religious
aspects—Christianity. I. Jones, David W. (David Wayne), 1973–
II. Köstenberger, Andreas J., 1957– God, marriage, and family. III. Title.
BS680.M35K67   2012
261.8'358—dc23   2011049812

CONTENTS

INTRODUCTION

For the first time in its history, Western civilization is confronted with the need to *define* the terms *marriage* and *family*. What until now has been considered a "normal" family, made up of a father, a mother, and a number of children, has in recent years increasingly begun to be viewed as one among several options, which can no longer claim to be the only or even superior form of ordering human relationships. The Judeo-Christian view of marriage and the family, with its roots in the Hebrew Scriptures, has to a significant extent been replaced with a set of values that prizes human rights, self-fulfillment, and pragmatic utility on an individual or societal level. It can rightly be said that marriage and the family are institutions under siege in our world today, and that with marriage and the family at risk, our very civilization is in crisis.

The current cultural crisis, however, is merely symptomatic of a deep-seated *spiritual* crisis that continues to gnaw at the foundations of our once-shared societal values. If God the Creator in fact instituted marriage and the family, as the Bible teaches, and if there is an evil being called Satan who wages war against God's creative purposes in this world, it should come as no surprise that the divine foundation of these institutions has come under massive attack in recent years. Ultimately, we human beings, whether we realize it or not, are involved in a cosmic spiritual conflict that pits God against Satan, with marriage and the family serving as a key arena in which spiritual and cultural battles are fought. If, then, the *cultural* crisis is symptomatic of an underlying *spiritual* crisis, the solution likewise must be spiritual, not merely cultural.

In *Marriage and the Family: Biblical Essentials*, we hope to point the way to this spiritual solution: a return to, and rebuilding of, the biblical foundation of marriage and the family. God's Word is not dependent on man's approval, and the Scriptures are not silent regarding the vital issues facing men and women and families today. In each of the important areas related to marriage and the family, the Bible offers satisfying instructions and wholesome remedies to the maladies afflicting our culture. The Scriptures record the divine institution of marriage and present a Christian theology of marriage and parenting. They offer insight for decision making regarding abortion, contraception, infertility, and adoption. They offer helpful guidance for those who are single or unmarried, and address the major threats to marriage and the family: homosexuality and divorce.

In the following pages, we will seek to determine what the Bible teaches on the various components of human relationships in an *integrative* manner: the nature of, and special issues related to, marriage and the family, childrearing, singleness, and so forth. Because the Bible is the Word of God, which is powerful and life-transforming, we know that those who are willing to be seriously engaged by Scripture will increasingly come to know and understand God's will for marriage and the family and be able to appropriate God's power in building strong Christian homes and families. This, in turn, will both increase God's honor and reputation in this world that he has made and provide the seasoning and illumination our world needs at this time of cultural ferment and crisis with regard to marriage and the family.

1

MARRIAGE IN THE BIBLE

What is God's plan for marriage? There is considerable confusion in contemporary culture regarding the nature of marriage. Only by returning to the biblical foundation for marriage and the family will we be able to rediscover God's good and perfect plan for humanity in this all-important area of our lives. In this chapter, we will survey all the major biblical passages regarding marriage in both Testaments.

MARRIAGE IN THE OLD TESTAMENT
Rooted in Creation (Genesis 1–3)
In exploring the biblical teaching on marriage, there is no more important paradigm than God's intended pattern for marriage presented in Genesis 1–3. Although Genesis was originally addressed to Israel's wilderness generation in preparation for entering the Promised Land, the early chapters of this book provide the parameters of the Creator's design for marriage in every age. This is reflected in Jesus's and Paul's teaching and applies to our own age as well.[1] Who is this God who had saved Israel from slavery in Egypt and had given the nation the law at Sinai? What are the foundational teachings on the family, societal structures, and sin?

The first three chapters of Genesis provide answers to these questions, initially from the vantage point of ancient Israel, but ultimately for every person who ever lived.[2] In Genesis 1–3, the God whom Israel had come to know as Redeemer and Lawgiver is revealed as the Creator of the universe, the all-powerful, all-wise, and eternal God who spoke everything there is into being. Marriage is shown to be rooted in God's creative act of making humanity in his image as male and female. Sin is depicted as the result of humanity's rebellion against the Creator at the instigation of Satan, himself a fallen creature, and as becoming so much a part of the human nature that people ever since the fall are by nature rebelling against their Creator and his plan for their lives.

The depiction of the original creation of man and woman and the subsequent fall of humanity in Genesis 1–3 centers on at least three very important clusters of principles: (1) the man and the woman are created in God's image *to rule the earth for God*; (2) the man is created first and is given *ultimate responsibility for the marriage relationship*, while the woman is placed alongside the man as his "suitable helper"; and (3) the fall of humanity entails *negative consequences* for both the man and the woman.

Created in God's Image to Rule the Earth for God

The fact that both men and women are created in the likeness and image of their Creator invests them with inestimable worth, dignity, and significance. God's image in the man and the woman has frequently been identified as conveying their possession of intelligence, a will, or emotions.[3] While this may be implied to some extent in Genesis 1:27, the immediate context develops the notion of the divine image in the man and the woman as indicating representative rule (see Ps. 8:6–8). This rule is the joint function of the man and the woman (note the plural pronouns in Gen. 1:28), although the man carries ultimate responsibility before God as the head of the woman.

Theologians have identified two aspects of the divine image in man: a *substantive* aspect (that is, an analogy between the nature of God and characteristics of humans), and a *functional* aspect (humans exercising the function of ruling the earth for God). While a substantive element cannot be ruled out, the functional component seems to reflect most accurately the emphasis in the biblical record.[4] This follows from the immediate context of Genesis 1:27, where creation is defined in terms of being fruitful and multiplying and subduing the earth (Gen. 1:28). The first man and the first woman were thus charged to exercise representative rule in part by *procreation*.

In this sense, then, human beings are "like God." Just as God rules over a large domain—the whole universe—so humanity is given charge of the entire earth to rule it for God. This also establishes the principle of *stewardship*: God, not the man and the woman, is ultimately owner of the created realm; the man and the woman are simply the divinely appointed caretakers. Moreover, this stewardship is a joint stewardship shared by the man and the woman. *Together* they are to exercise it according to the will and for the glory of God. *Together* they are to multiply and be stewards of the children God will give them. And *together* they are to subdue the earth by a division of labor that assigns to the man the primary responsibility to provide for his wife and children, and to the woman the care for and nurture of her family.

The Man's Ultimate Responsibility for the Marriage and the Wife's Role as His "Suitable Helper"

The apostle Paul's comments on Genesis 1–3 repeatedly root the man's primary responsibility in both the family and the church in the fact that he was *created first*. Not only does Paul draw attention to the fact that the man was created first, but he also points out that it is not the man who was made for the woman, but the woman for the man (1 Cor. 11:9; see Gen. 2:18, 20) and from the man (1 Cor. 11:8, 12; see Gen. 2:22). Moreover, the man was the one who received the divine command (Gen. 2:16–17), was presented with the woman (Gen. 2:22), and named the woman with a name derived from his own (Gen. 2:23; see 3:20), which also implies his authority.[5]

While Genesis 1 simply notes the creation of man as male and female in God's image, Genesis 2 provides further detail on the exact order and orientation of the creation of man and woman. At the beginning of human history, God made the first man, endowed him with life, and placed him in a garden (Gen. 2:7–8, 15). Moreover, God addressed to the man certain moral commands (Gen. 2:16–17). Prior to the creation of the woman, the man had already begun exercising the divine mandate to subdue the earth, by naming the animals (Gen. 2:19–20). In order to supply his need for companionship, God created the woman to be Adam's wife.

God's creation of Eve demonstrates that his plan for Adam's marriage, and all subsequent marriages, involves a monogamous heterosexual relationship.[6] God only made *one* helper for Adam, and she was *female.* What is more, it was *God* who perceived Adam's aloneness and created the woman. The biblical text gives no indication that Adam was even conscious of being alone. Rather, God takes the initiative in fashioning a compatible human companion for the man. For this reason we can confidently say that marriage is God's idea and that it was God who made the woman as a "suitable helper" for the man (Gen. 2:18, 20 NIV).

But what is the force of the expression "suitable helper"? On the one hand, the woman is *congenial* to the man in a way that none of the animals are (Gen. 2:19–20; she is "bone of [his] bones and flesh of [his] flesh," Gen. 2:23); on the other hand, she is placed alongside the man as his *associate* or *assistant.* On a personal level, she will provide for the man's need for *companionship* (Gen. 2:18). In relation to God's mandate for humanity to be fruitful and multiply and to fill the earth and subdue it (Gen. 1:28), the woman is a suitable partner both in *procreation* (becoming "one flesh" with him, Gen. 2:24) and in the earth's *domestication* (Gen. 1:28).[7] Her role is distinct from the man's, yet unique and exceedingly significant. While assigned to the man as his "helper" and thus placed under his overall charge, the woman is his partner in ruling the earth for God.

There are, however, those who would blur the biblical roles of man and woman, or deny the wife's subordination. Yet nowhere is the *man* called the *woman's* "helper." Thus equality and distinctness, complementarity and submission/authority must be held in fine balance. The man and the woman are jointly charged with ruling the earth representatively for God, yet they are not to do so as "unisex" creatures, but each as fulfilling their God-ordained, gender-specific roles. In fact, since these functional differences are part of the Creator's design, it is only when men and women embrace their God-ordained roles that they will be truly fulfilled and God's creational wisdom will be fully displayed and exalted.[8]

The Fall of Humanity and Its Consequences

The fall witnesses a complete reversal of the roles God assigns to the man and the woman. Rather than God's being in charge, with the man, helped by the woman, ruling creation for him, Satan, in the form of a serpent, approaches the woman, who draws the man with her into rebellion against the Creator. This does not imply that the woman is more susceptible to temptation than the man. It does indicate, however, that God's plan is to have the man, not the woman, assume ultimate responsibility for the couple, extending leadership and protection to his female counterpart. The man, by his absence, or at least acquiescence (Gen. 3:6: "her husband who was with her"; see Gen. 3:17), shares in the woman's culpability; and she, by failing to consult with her God-given protector and provider, fails to respect the divine pattern of marriage. In the end, it is the *man*, not the woman, who is primarily held responsible for the rebellious act (Gen. 3:9; see Gen. 3:17; Rom. 5:12–14), though the consequences of the fall extend to the man and the woman alike, affecting their respective primary spheres.

In the case of the woman, consequences ensue in the realm of childbearing and the relationship with her husband. Regarding childbearing, the woman will experience physical pain. As far as the woman's relationship with her husband is concerned, loving harmony will be replaced by a pattern of struggle in which the woman seeks to exert control over her husband, who responds by asserting his authority—often in an ungodly manner by either passively forcing her into action or actively dominating her (Gen. 3:16; see 4:7).[9] The man, in turn, will henceforth have trouble in fulfilling God's command to subdue the earth (see Gen. 1:28). He must extract the fruit of the land from thorns and thistles and eat his bread by the sweat of his brow (Gen. 3:17–19). In the end, both the man and the woman will die (Gen. 3:19, 22).

Nevertheless, God continues to provide for the human couple, clothing them (Gen. 3:21) and, more significantly, predicting a time when the woman's seed—the promised Messiah—will bruise the Serpent's offspring on the head (Gen. 3:15). In the meantime, however, the couple is expelled from the garden (Gen. 3:24) as a sign that their rebellion against the Creator had met with severe sanctions that would cast an ominous shadow on their marriage during their sojourn on earth from that time onward.

DEVELOPMENTS IN THE HISTORY OF ISRAEL

Marital Roles according to the Old Testament

Even subsequent to the fall, God's creation design for marriage continues to provide the norm and standard for God's expectations for male-female relationships. Based on the foundational treatment of Genesis 1 and 2, subsequent chapters of the Hebrew Scriptures provide information on the roles and responsibilities of husbands and wives toward each other. While the reality often fell short of the ideal, this does not alter the fact that the standards that were in place for Old Testament couples and believers were grounded in the pre-fall ideal.

The Role and Responsibilities of Husbands toward Their Wives

The Old Testament does not contain an explicit "job description" for husbands. Nevertheless, it is possible to infer some of the major responsibilities of husbands toward their wives from various portions of the Hebrew Scriptures. Among these are the following: (1) to love and cherish his wife and to treat her with respect and dignity; (2) to bear primary responsibility for the marriage union and ultimate authority over the family; and (3) to provide food, clothing, and other necessities for his wife.

First, a man is to *love and cherish his wife and to treat her with respect and dignity*. As one endowed with the image of God, commissioned as the man's suitable helper and partner in filling the earth and subduing it, and as his complement provided by God (Gen. 1:27–28), his wife is worthy of full respect and dignity and is to be cherished as his trusted companion and friend. As the foundational creation narrative stipulates, in order to be united to his wife a man is to leave his father and mother and hold fast to his wife, and they will establish a new family unit (Gen. 2:24). Part of their marital union will be the procreation of offspring (Gen. 1:28).

Second, from the man's creation prior to the woman, later biblical writers (such as Paul, see 1 Cor. 11:8–9) rightly infer that his is the *primary responsibility for the marriage union and ultimate authority over his family* including his wife. Consider the following indicators in the opening chapters of Genesis: the man's responsibilities prior to the creation of the woman (Gen. 2:19–20); the man's direct commission by God to keep the garden of Eden and not to eat from the tree of the knowledge of good and evil (Gen. 2:15–17); and the man's naming of the woman (Gen. 2:23). While the fall distorted the way in which men exercised their headship in subsequent generations (Gen. 3:16b), men were not to avoid their God-given responsibility to be in charge of their marriage and family and all that this entailed. The man's primary responsibility and ultimate authority is consistently seen in the Old Testament pattern of male heads of households, a system which is commonly called "patriarchy" but which is better described as "patricentrism."[10]

Third, a husband is to provide his wife with food, clothing, and other necessities. While the context is that of a man's responsibilities toward concubines or slave wives, the most important discussion of the husband's duties in this regard is found in

Exodus 21:10. This passage stipulates that, "If he [the man] takes another wife to himself, he shall not diminish her *food*, her *clothing*, or her *marital rights*." According to this passage, the husband's obligations toward his wife (and concubines or slave girls) are delineated as involving the provision of food, clothing, and marital rights respectively. This circumscribes the husband's responsibility to provide his wife with peace, permanence, and security (Ruth 1:9 speaks of "rest").

The Role and Responsibilities of Wives toward Their Husbands

Wives' roles and responsibilities toward their husbands were considered to be essentially threefold in ancient Israel: (1) presenting her husband with children (especially male ones); (2) managing the household; and (3) providing her husband with companionship.

Regarding the first wifely duty, that of *presenting her husband with children* (particularly sons), people in ancient times married in order to have children. In keeping with the belief that fathers lived on in their children, bearing a child was considered to be an act performed by a wife for her husband.[11] Bearing a son was the noblest contribution a wife could make to her husband and her household. Failure to do so, on the other hand, was viewed as a disgrace. Hence, in the book of Genesis we see that Rachel is desperate that she has not yet borne Jacob any children, and when God later enables her to conceive, she interprets this as God having taken away her reproach (Gen. 30:1, 23).

Second, wives were to *manage their household*, fulfilling the divine mandate of keeping the garden of Eden prior to the fall of humanity (Gen. 1:28; see 2:15). The wife's responsibilities in ancient Israel in this regard included cooking, clothing the family, tending the garden, and harvesting grain. Yet while there was a general division of labor along those lines, the boundaries were not rigid, and some of these activities were not limited exclusively to women. Abraham (Gen. 18:1–8), Lot (Gen. 19:3), and Esau (Gen. 27:30–31) all are shown to be involved in meal preparations in the

Old Testament. Wives also were to supervise household servants involved in domestic chores.

Third, in keeping with God's original purpose for creating her (see Gen. 2:18), the wife was to *provide companionship* for her husband. While legally his subordinate, ideally the wife served as her husband's confidante and trusted friend (see Mal. 2:14). The mutual trust and intimacy characteristic of an ideal marriage is celebrated in the Song of Solomon (e.g., 2:16; 6:3; 7:10).

Violations of God's Ideal for Marriage in Ancient Israel
Polygamy

The history of Israel witnesses repeated instances of polygamy (or, more precisely, polygyny). While it certainly was within the Creator's prerogative and power to make more than one wife for the man, God intentionally made only Eve, revealing to Adam his plan with the words, "A man [singular] shall leave his father and his mother and hold fast to his wife [singular], and they shall become one flesh" (Gen. 2:24). As could be expected, though, after the fall of humanity, God's ideal of monogamy was not consistently upheld.[12] Within six generations, barely after Adam had died, the Bible records that "Lamech took two wives" (Gen. 4:19).

While polygamy was *never normative* among the followers of Israel's God, Scripture reveals that it was indeed a recurrent event, even among some of its most important individuals (both reportedly godly and ungodly). Despite this trend, the Old Testament clearly communicates that the practice of having multiple wives was a departure from God's plan for marriage. This is conveyed not only in Scripture verses that seem univocally to prohibit polygamy (see Lev. 18:18; Deut. 17:17), but also from the sin and general disorder that polygamy produced in the lives of those who engaged in the practice. For example, the Old Testament reports disruptive favoritism in the polygamous marriages of Jacob (Gen. 29:30), Elkanah (1 Sam. 1:4–5), and Rehoboam (2 Chron. 11:21). In addition, jealousy was a frequent problem between the competing wives of Abraham (Gen. 21:9–10), Jacob (Gen. 30:14–16), and Elkanah (1 Sam. 1:6). Moreover, Scripture reports that Solomon's foreign wives "turned away his heart after other gods" (1 Kings 11:4), a violation of the first commandment, and David's multiple marriages led to incest and murder among his progeny. The sin and disorder produced by polygamy, then, is further testimony to the goodness of God's monogamous design of marriage as first revealed in the marriage of Adam and Eve in the garden of Eden. Not only is polygamy nowhere in the Old Testament spoken of with approval (see Ex. 21:10–11; Deut. 21:15–17), but many passages clearly uphold monogamy as the continuing ideal (e.g., Prov. 12:4; 18:22; 19:14; 31:10–31; Ps. 128:3; Ezek. 16:8).

Divorce

Another component of God's design for marriage that Old Testament Israel regularly compromised is the durability of marriage. The opening chapters of Genesis make clear that God designed marriage to be *permanent*. This is evident in the paradigmatic description of marriage in Genesis 2:24: "A man shall leave his father and his mother and *hold fast* to his wife, and *they shall become one flesh*."[13]

Again, however, the Old Testament indicates that many did not respect that God's plan involved the durability of marriage. Divorce was a serious problem early on in the history of Israel. In the Mosaic code, it was stipulated that a priest could not marry a divorcée (even if she was not the guilty party; Lev. 21:7; see Lev. 21:14). In an attempt to bridle sins stemming from divorce, Mosaic legislation prohibited a man from remarrying a woman whom he had divorced and who subsequently had married another man (even if her second husband had died, Deut. 24:1–4). The reason for this was that by her second marriage "she has been defiled" (Deut. 24:4), perhaps indicating that illegitimate remarriage after divorce amounts to adultery. Moreover, the Old Testament records several examples of divorces and attests to the general practice of divorce among the Hebrews (Ezra 9–10; Neh. 13:23–31; Mal. 2:14–16).

Despite the presence of divorce in the history of Israel, however, the Old Testament confirms that durability continued to be a component of God's design for marriage. This can be seen in that the Mosaic legislation seems specifically to *forbid* divorce if the wife was a virgin at the time the marriage was consummated (see Deut. 22:19, 29). In addition, it is evident that God does not approve of divorce, for the Old Testament on several occasions uses the analogy of divorce to describe Israel's spiritual apostasy (see Isa. 50:1; Jer. 3:8), and the prophet Malachi makes clear that God does not approve of divorce motivated by hatred (Mal. 2:16).

Adultery

Another way in which God's ideal for marriage was compromised in the history of Israel was by way of adultery.[14] While it could be argued that fidelity was Adam's only option, his lack of an opportunity to commit adultery does not diminish the fact that fidelity is an inherent component of God's pattern for marriage: "A man shall leave his father and his mother and *hold fast* to his wife, and they shall become one flesh" (Gen. 2:24). As with the principle of monogamy, however, after the fall of humankind the Old Testament reports that numerous individuals struggled to be faithful to their marriage partners.

Perhaps the best-known incident of adultery recorded in the Old Testament is David's adultery with Bathsheba and the consequent murder of her husband, Uriah (2 Samuel 11). Other instances of marital infidelity abound in the history of Israel. There are, to name a few, Reuben's adultery with Bilhah (Gen. 35:22; see 49:3–4), the adultery of the Levite's concubine (Judg. 19:1–2), and Hosea's wife Gomer's adultery (Hos. 3:1). Despite these instances of adultery in the history of Israel, however, the Old Testament reiterates in numerous places that God's ideal for marriage is *fidelity*. For instance, the seventh commandment directed God's people in no uncertain terms, "You shall not commit adultery" (Ex. 20:14; Deut. 5:18). The sexual laws in the Holiness Code plainly stipulated, "You shall not lie sexually with your neighbor's wife" (Lev. 18:20), setting the penalty for adultery as death (Lev. 20:10; see Num. 5:11–31; Deut. 22:22). Moreover, the book of Proverbs repeatedly classifies adultery as both foolish and dangerous (Prov. 2:16–19; 5:3–22; 6:32–33; 7:5–23; 9:13–18; 22:14; 23:27–28; 30:20).

What is more, the Lord frequently used the analogy of physical adultery to depict his displeasure over the spiritual adultery of Israel when they departed from him, their first love, in order to pursue other gods (Jer. 3:8–9; Ezek. 16:32, 38; Hos. 1:1–3:5). In short, then, although many in the history of Israel did not adhere to God's design of fidelity within marriage, the Old Testament is clear that the Lord's standard did not change. God expected his people to be faithful—both to their spouse and to him—and was clearly offended when they were not.

Homosexuality

Heterosexuality is an unequivocal component of the Creator's design for marriage. Yet after the fall of humanity, the Old Testament indicates that the principle of heterosexuality was often violated through same-sex relations. Examples include many of the inhabitants of the cities of the plain, Sodom and Gomorrah (Gen. 19:1–29), the Gibeonites in the days of the judges (Judg. 19:1–21:25), as well as numerous other unnamed lawbreakers in the history of Israel (1 Kings 14:24; 15:12; 22:46; 2 Kings 23:7; Job 36:14).

In spite of these offenses, however, the Old Testament makes clear that the principle of heterosexuality, established at creation, continues to be an integral part of God's design for marriage. This is testified to by the severity of the punishment prescribed for homosexuality—death (Lev. 20:13)—by the presentation of heterosexuality as normative (Prov. 5:18–19; Eccl. 9:9; Song 1–8), and by the fate of individuals in the history of Israel who engaged in homosexual activity.

The idea of a homosexual marriage is not only contrary to specific biblical injunctions concerning same-sex intercourse (see Lev. 18:22; 20:13; Deut. 23:17) but also runs counter to the Creator's design for marriage. Heterosexuality—not homosexuality—is plainly in view in God's law of marriage: "A *man* [masculine] shall leave his father and his mother and hold fast to his *wife* [feminine], and they shall become one flesh" (Gen. 2:24). What is more, this is the only possible arrangement for marriage, as the Creator has commanded and expects married couples to "be fruitful and multiply and fill the earth" (Gen. 1:28).

Since homosexuality involves same-sex intercourse that cannot lead to procreation, it is unnatural and cannot logically entail the possibility of marriage. Indeed, even among the animals, the writer of Genesis repeatedly notes that God made each species male and female, "according to their kinds," for the express purpose of procreation (Gen. 1:21, 24, 25). Moreover, since an aspect of humanity's representative rule over and subduing of the earth for God is procreation (Gen. 1:27–28), and procreation is impossible between two males or two females, homosexuality militates not only against God's design for marriage but against his created order as well.

Sterility

Fertility is yet another essential part of God's design for marriage of which certain individuals fell short in Old Testament times. Fertility is certainly entailed in God's command to Adam and Eve; "be fruitful and multiply" (Gen. 1:28) is, incidentally, the first command God gave to human beings. Indeed, in the Bible fruitfulness in marriage is repeatedly described as a virtue to be sought after and is viewed as a blessing once obtained (see Ex. 23:26; Deut. 7:14; Ps. 113:9; 127:4–5; 128:3–4). Moreover, certain elements of the Old Testament law appear to be crafted with the intent of furthering the fruitfulness of marriage. Examples include a newlywed soldier being given a year off "to be happy with his wife whom he has taken" (Deut. 24:5) and the institution of levirate marriage that had as its goal the production of offspring for a deceased relative (Deut. 25:5–10). Conversely, the Old Testament views barrenness as a reproach (see Gen. 30:1, 22–23; Isa. 4:1; 47:9; 49:21).

Despite the importance placed on fertility in the Hebrew Scriptures, the fact remains that numerous couples in the history of Israel experienced difficulty conceiving children. One important difference between one's lack of fertility and one's failure to implement other components of God's design for marriage is that sterility is not usually a conscious choice. Nevertheless, in the Old Testament sterility is sometimes presented as a curse stemming from personal sin, as in the case of Abimelech's wives (Gen. 20:17–18) and David's first wife, Michal (2 Sam. 6:23). On other occasions, sterility is presented as a simple fact of nature, as in the case of the three mothers of the Hebrew race—Sarah (Gen. 11:30), Rebekah (Gen. 25:21), and Rachel (Gen. 30:1)—as well as Manoah's wife (Judg. 13:2), Hannah (1 Sam. 1:2), and the Shunammite who aided Elisha (2 Kings 4:14).

While the Bible gives no explicit directives on how to overcome sterility, a common denominator among many of those in Scripture who were at one time fruitless but later became fruitful is prayer. For example, God answered prayers for fertility offered by Abraham (Gen. 15:2–5; 20:17), Isaac (Gen. 25:21), Leah (Gen. 30:17), Rachel (Gen. 30:22), and Hannah (1 Sam. 1:9–20). These answered prayers, as well as the Lord's general multiplication of his people in fulfillment of the Abrahamic covenant, are further testimony to the fact that fertility is an essential component of God's design for marriage and is possible for those who seek God regarding it.

Dilution of Gender Distinctions

Complementarity, which includes the notion of equal worth but differing roles for the sexes, is an essential and foundational part of God's design of marriage. However, as is evident from the other marital distortions mentioned above, the history of Israel features several instances where the principle of complementarity was not observed. Individuals who engaged in homosexuality or who purposefully avoided fruitfulness (e.g., Onan, Gen. 38:8–10) cannot be described as having behaved in a manner that is fully consistent with the God-ordained pattern of complementarity.

In addition, the Old Testament features a number of individuals who clearly and specifically abandoned their God-ordained gender roles, some without participating in other marital distortions. For instance, men who failed in the leadership of their home (at least on occasion) include Adam, Eli, David, and Ahaz, and examples of women who (at least at times) were not "suitable helpers" within their families include Eve, Bathsheba, Jezebel, and Athaliah, among others.

Despite these examples of distortion of the Creator's design of gender roles, even after the fall, the Old Testament repeatedly confirms the fact that complementarity is part of God's plan for marriage. Equal worth of husbands and wives is seen in a number of different spheres: legal parity in regard to parental obedience (Ex. 20:12; 21:15, 17; Lev. 20:9; Deut. 5:16); economic privileges that allowed for daughters and wives to inherit property (Num. 27:1–11; 36:1–9; see Prov. 31:13–18, 24); and liberty for both sexes to have personal spiritual encounters (Judg. 13:2–25), experience answered prayer (1 Sam. 1:9–20), engage in public worship (Neh. 8:2), and perhaps even to participate in the prophetic office (Ex. 15:20; Judg. 4:4; 2 Kings 22:14; Neh. 6:14).

At the same time, the Lord's design for marriage in the Old Testament includes important functional differences for the sexes as well. In addition to the Lord's specific confirmation of Adam's headship after the fall (Gen. 3:16), complementary gender roles as established at creation are evident in the Old Testament narratives recounting the marriages of the patriarchs (e.g., Abraham: Gen. 18:12, where Sarah calls Abraham "my lord"; see 1 Pet. 3:5–6) and godly kings of Israel (e.g., David in 1 Sam. 25:40–42; 1 Kings 1:16, 31). King Lemuel's description of a virtuous wife as an industrious homemaker under her husband's authority (Prov. 31:10–31) also reflects the complementary pattern instituted in Genesis 2.[15] As with the other components in God's design for marriage, it is clear that the history of Israel did not alter the Lord's plan for these institutions.

GLIMPSES OF THE IDEAL (WISDOM LITERATURE)
The Excellent Wife (Proverbs 31)
The book of Proverbs concludes with an acrostic poem (moving from the first to the last letter of the Hebrew alphabet) extolling the virtues of the excellent wife whose worth to her husband surpasses that of great material wealth (Prov. 31:10–31). At the heart of the poem (vv. 20–27) appears to be a chiasm (i.e., an ABB'A' pattern), climaxing in the reference to the woman's husband being respected at the city gates (v. 23). This may indicate that the respect that the man receives is in large part related to the noble character and accomplishments of his wife.

Some have commented that this woman must have been phenomenal, since on the one hand it is said that she rises early in the morning (Prov. 31:15) and on the other that her lamp does not go out at night (Prov. 31:18)! When did this woman sleep? Rather than viewing these qualities as existing in a woman all at one time, depicting a day in the life of the ideal woman, one may view these attributes as having developed over a period of time and as being exhibited in a woman's life during different occasions and seasons of life. Indeed, the excellent wife of Proverbs 31 displays many virtues that remain relevant for women aspiring to be godly wives today. The Proverbs 31 woman:

- Is a major asset to her husband (vv. 10, 11)
- Is a trusted companion (v. 11)
- Is for and not against her husband; she has his well-being and best interests at heart (v. 12)

- Is industrious and hardworking (vv. 13, 27)
- Procures and prepares food for her entire household (vv. 14, 15)
- Rises early (v. 15)
- Locates and purchases real estate (v. 16)
- Reinvests extra earnings from her home business (v. 16)
- Is vigorous, energetic (vv. 17, 25)
- Produces clothes for her family and as merchandise (vv. 13, 18–19, 21–22, 24)
- Is kind to the poor, reaches out in mercy to the needy (v. 20)
- Ensures that she and her children are properly and finely dressed (vv. 21–22)
- Contributes to others' respect for her husband and oversees her household so he can devote himself to a role of leadership in the community (vv. 23, 27)
- Is ready for the future and prepares for eventualities (vv. 21, 25)
- Displays wisdom in speech, teaching of kindness (v. 26)
- Is praised by her children and husband (vv. 28–29, 31)
- Is God-fearing rather than relying on her physical beauty (v. 30)

While some might find this ideal unattainable, it is a worthy goal to which women today may aspire. This picture is consistent with God's overall design for women as supportive partners of their husbands. However, this kind of woman clearly breaks the stereotype of a woman who is "confined to the home" or diminished in her personhood. She is a woman of great resourcefulness who is a source of strength and inestimable blessing to her husband and children. Who would not want to have a wife and mother aspiring to such a role model?

The Beauty of Sex in Marriage (The Song of Solomon)

In the midst of the deterioration evident during the course of Israel's history, there is one other bright spot in the Hebrew canon: the Song of Solomon. On the basis of the notion that God established marriage, including the physical union of husband and wife (Gen. 2:18–25, esp. Gen. 2:24–25: "one flesh . . . both naked and . . . not ashamed"), the Song of Solomon celebrates the beauty of marital love, including its intimate sexual expression.[16]

Not only does the Song of Solomon contribute to the Hebrew (and Christian) canon a collection of love poems celebrating the strength and passion of married love (including sex), the book also anticipates the restoration of the relationship between the first man and the first woman, Adam and Eve, which was ruptured by the fall. Subsequent to the fall, the judgment pronounced on the woman included that her desire would be for her husband (Gen. 3:16), which in all likelihood conveys the woman's sinful desire to manipulate and control her husband rather than to lovingly submit to him (see Gen. 4:7).[17]

In the third and only other instance of the term translated "desire" in these passages, Song of Solomon 7:10, the woman exclaims, "I am my beloved's, and his desire is for me." Rather than the woman's desire being illegitimately to control her husband, a restoration of the original state is envisioned in which the husband's desire will be for his wife. Once again, the woman gladly rests in the assurance that she is her husband's, and the husband does not dominate his wife but desires her. This kind of love signifies a return to paradise. As in the original garden, the man and the woman will be able to be "both naked and . . . not ashamed" (Gen. 2:25).

MARRIAGE IN THE NEW TESTAMENT
No Longer Two, but One: Jesus's High View of Marriage

Jesus's teaching on the requirements of discipleship regularly subordinated one's kinship ties to the obligations of the kingdom. However, while our Lord had much to say about people's need to give first priority to Jesus's call to discipleship, he provided comparatively little instruction on marriage. Doubtless the major reason for this is that Jesus, like his contemporaries, assumed the validity of the divine pattern for marriage set forth in the opening chapters of Genesis.

When questioned about divorce, Jesus affirmed the permanent nature of marriage in no uncertain terms. Adducing both foundational Old Testament texts, Genesis 1:27 and 2:24, he asserted, "So they [husband and wife] are no longer two, but one flesh. Therefore what God has joined together, let no one separate" (Matt. 19:6 NIV). This makes clear that Jesus considered marriage to be *a sacred bond between a man and a woman, established by and entered into before God.*

While Jesus held a very high view of marriage, however, his teaching on natural family ties provides important parameters, placing it within the larger context of God's kingdom. The culmination of this development will be reached in the eternal state where people will no longer marry but will be like the angels (Matt. 22:30). Thus, Jesus lays the groundwork for Paul's teaching that "from now on those who have wives should live as if they do not . . . for this world in its present form is passing away" (1 Cor. 7:29, 31 NIV).

Submission and Sensitivity: Peter's Message to Husbands and Wives (1 Pet. 3:1–7)

Peter's comments on the marriage relationship are penned in the context of believers suffering at the hands of unbelievers, specifically, believing wives called to live with unbelieving husbands. Peter's general rule of conduct is submission "for the Lord's sake to every human institution" (1 Pet. 2:13), including government (1 Pet. 2:13–17), authorities at work (1 Pet. 2:18), and at home (1 Pet. 3:1). In the case of work relationships, submission is urged not only to superiors who are "good and gentle but also to the unjust" (1 Pet. 2:18). Wives, likewise, are to be submissive to unbelieving husbands (1 Pet. 3:1).[18]

In all of this, Christ has set the example (1 Pet. 2:21), all the way to the cross (1 Pet. 2:24). Marriage, as well as other human relationships, is thus set in the larger framework of a believer's Christian testimony in the surrounding unbelieving world. While there is no guarantee (see 1 Cor. 7:16), believing wives are to work and pray that their husbands "may be won without a word by the conduct of their wives—when they see your respectful and pure conduct" (1 Pet. 3:1–2; see 1 Cor. 7:12–14). Such wives are to cultivate inner, spiritual beauty (1 Pet. 3:4), being submissive to their husbands as Sarah was to Abraham. They are called to do so even when their husbands' directives are not informed by a regenerate mind and heart, as long as this does not involve sin (1 Pet. 3:3–6; see, e.g., Genesis 20).

In the sole verse addressed to husbands, Peter admirably balances the recognition of distinctions between the marital partners and the notion of their equality in Christ. On the one hand, wives are called "the weaker vessel" with whom husbands are to live in an understanding way. Yet on the other hand, wives are called "heirs with you [their husbands]" of the gracious gift of life (1 Pet. 3:7). The reference to removing any obstacles for joint marital prayer closes Peter's instruction to married couples.

Paul's Vision for Marriage
Fulfilling One's Marital Obligations (1 Cor. 7:2–5)

Paul's pronouncements on marriage in his first letter to the Corinthians are part of his response to a letter sent to him by the Corinthians, in which they had requested that the apostle rule on several controversial issues (1 Cor. 16:17). In his response, the apostle takes a strong stand against a false *asceticism* that values singleness as more spiritual than marriage (1 Cor. 7:1). Suppressing their physical functions for the sake of spiritual advancement, the proponents of this teaching apparently called on those who were married to refrain from sexual intercourse with their spouse or even encouraged them to divorce him or her in order to pursue an allegedly higher, sexless spirituality.

While 1 Corinthians 7 is often discussed in the context of Paul's high valuation of singleness, it is worthy of note that the same chapter also contains a very strong affirmation of marriage. In 1 Corinthians 7:2–5, Paul urges the husband and the wife not to withdraw from normal marital sexual relations but to fulfill their sexual obligations toward their marriage partner. This reveals Paul's high view of marriage and contradicts the misguided spirituality promoted by some in the Corinthian congregation.

Marriage an Honorable State (1 Tim. 2:15; 4:1–4)

First Timothy contains a very strong reaffirmation of the centrality of marriage in the age of Christ. As in Corinth, some in Ephesus (the destination of 1 Timothy) were teaching that Christians ought to abstain from marriage. Paul counters this teaching with extremely strong language, contending that those "who forbid marriage" (1 Tim. 4:3) were "devoting themselves to deceitful spirits and teachings of demons" (1 Tim. 4:1). In contrast, he maintains that "everything created by God [including marriage] is good, and nothing is to be rejected if it is received with thanksgiving" (1 Tim. 4:4).

Earlier in the letter, Paul affirms "childbearing" (i.e., a woman's devotion to her domestic and familial duties, including childrearing) as a vital part of a woman's life of faith (1 Tim. 2:15) and calls candidates for both overseer and deacon to be faithful to their wives (1 Tim. 3:2, 12; see Titus 1:6) and to manage their households well, keeping their children submissive (1 Tim. 3:4; see Titus 1:6). In the former passage, Paul adduces both the Genesis creation and fall narratives (see 1 Tim. 2:13–14), which indicates that he views marriage as a divine creation ordinance that, though affected by the fall, continues to obtain in the age of Christ.

All Things under One Head: The Roles of
Husband and Wife (Eph. 5:21–33)

Paul's most thorough treatment of marriage is found in his letter to the Ephesians. Read *in the context of the entire letter*, it becomes clear that Paul set marriage within the larger context of God's final restoration of all things under the headship of Christ. At the very outset Paul affirms God's overarching purpose for humanity (including married couples) in the age of Christ: "to bring all things in heaven and on earth under one head, even Christ" (Eph. 1:10 NIV). This establishes Christ as the focal point of God's end-time program, as well as the head (Eph. 1:22), not only over the church (Eph. 1:22) but over every authority, in the present as well as the coming age (Eph. 1:21). Clearly, Christ's headship here conveys the notion of supreme authority, not merely that of provision or nurture. As the exalted Lord, Christ is the head, and all things are subjected to him (see Phil. 2:9–11).

The first important lesson for marriage from Paul's teaching in Ephesians is therefore that the marriage relationship must be seen within the compass of God's larger purposes, that is, the bringing of "all things in heaven and on earth together under one head, even Christ" (Eph. 1:10 NIV). This includes spiritual powers who will be fully submitted to Christ (Eph. 1:21); the bringing together of Jews and Gentiles in one entity, the church (Eph. 2:11–22; 3:6–13); the restoration of creation (see Rom. 8:18–25), which men, as divine image bearers, are currently working to subdue (Gen. 1:28); and, most relevant for our present purposes, the restoration of the male-female marriage relationship as realized by Spirit-filled, committed Christian believers, who overcome the cursed struggle of manipulation and dominance (see Gen. 3:16) in the power of Christ and relate to each other in proper submission and Christlike love.

Paul continues to develop these important truths in the following chapters of his letter. In Ephesians 2, he affirms that believers (and hence also Christian husbands and wives) were once in the realm of Satan, but now they have been made alive in Christ, by grace (Eph. 2:5). They have been raised and exalted *with him*, participating in his victory over Satan (Eph. 2:6). God's end-time plan to bring together all things in and under Christ is nowhere more evident than in his inclusion of the Gentiles in the community of believers together with believing Jews (Eph. 2:11–22; 3:6).[19] This Paul calls a salvation-historical "mystery," hidden in the past in God's own purposes, but now brought into the open and unpacked by the apostle himself.

At the close of his discussion of believers' spiritual blessings in Christ, Paul prays that Christ would live in their hearts by faith and that, rooted and established in love, they would know his love in their lives (Eph. 3:17, 19). The fact that Paul begins his prayer with a reference to God "the Father, from whom every family in heaven and on earth is named" (Eph. 3:14–15) underscores the relevance of Paul's prayer not only for believers in general but *for married couples and families in particular*. Here, the Creator is identified as the one who both established marriage and has rightful jurisdiction over it and whose rule over families extends to earthly families as well as heavenly realities.

The second half of the letter is given to an exposition of the new life in Christ that believers are to enjoy in the unity of the "body of Christ," the church. They are to walk in a manner worthy of their calling, give preference to one another in love, and preserve spiritual unity in peace (Eph. 4:1–3; see 4:4–6). God has given spiritual gifts and instituted various ministries in the church to equip believers for ministry. In all this, his goal is the "perfect man" (Eph. 4:13 NKJV) who speaks the truth in love and in all things grows into Christ, who is the head (Eph. 4:13–16). Paul then contrasts the old self, with its independence, lack of submission to authority, and bondage to passions and lusts, with the new self, which is characterized by proper submission, respect for authority, and love. Becoming a Christian is like putting off old clothes and putting on new ones (Eph. 4:22, 24; see Col. 3:9–10): there must be a marked, noticeable change in spirit and behavior—including the realm of marriage and the family.

In the context immediately preceding Paul's teaching on marital roles, he exhorts believers to live lives of love in keeping with the love of Christ who gave his life as a sacrifice for them (Eph. 5:1–2; see 5:25). Conversely, there must be no sexual immorality (*porneia*; Eph. 5:3; see 1 Cor. 6:15–16). As God's end-time community, the church (and hence every believer) ought to be filled with the Spirit (Eph. 5:18).[20] In the first instance, this Spirit-filling refers to congregational worship (Eph. 5:19–20). Paul then relates Spirit-filling to the marriage relationship (Eph. 5:21–24). *Being properly submitted* (Eph. 5:21, 22) is thus a mark of Spirit-filling, in contrast to believers' previous lifestyle, which was characterized by rebellion toward authority.

The second important lesson for married couples, then, is that the instructions for wives and husbands (as well as those for parents/children and slaves/masters later on) are *directed to Spirit-filled believers*. In the following verses, Paul cites models for both wives and husbands to emulate: for wives, the church in her submission to Christ (Eph. 5:24); for husbands, Christ's sacrificial love for the church, resulting in her cleansing, holiness, and purity (Eph. 5:25–28). Later, Paul will add a second, commonsense analogy from the nature of things, appealing to self-interest: everyone loves one's own body; therefore, in light of the one-flesh union between husbands and wives, if husbands love their wives, this is tantamount to husbands' loving themselves (Eph. 5:29–30).

On the basis of Ephesians 5:21 ("submitting *to one another* out of reverence for Christ"), some argue that Paul does not teach the submission of wives to their husbands *only* but *also* that of husbands to their wives in "mutual submission." However, we must not stop reading at 5:21 but glean from the following verses what is Paul's definition of "submitting to one another." It is clear that the answer is (our third important principle on marriage from Paul's letter to the Ephesians) that *wives are to submit to their husbands* who are called the "head" of their wives as Christ is the head of the church (Eph. 5:22–24) while *husbands are to love their wives with the sacrificial love of Christ* (Eph. 5:25–30). This runs counter to the notion of "mutual submission."[21]

A comparison with Ephesians 1:22 and 4:15 further supports the notion, fourth, that *"headship" entails not merely nurture* (though it does that; see Eph. 5:29) *but also a position of authority.*

This authoritative position of the man is a function of God's sovereign creative will (and perhaps reflective of God's authority in light of his revelation of himself as Father), not of intrinsic merit or worth on his part. Hence the husband's leadership, as well as the wife's submission, is to be exercised within the orbit of grace rather than legalism or coercion. Note also that the Colossian parallel, "Wives, submit to your husbands, as is fitting in the Lord" (Col. 3:18), sums up the entirety of Paul's counsel to Christian wives with regard to their marital disposition (no word about "mutual submission" here).[22]

That wives are called to recognize and respect proper authority over them is not unique to them. Men, too, must submit to Christ, local church leadership and discipline, the civil authorities, and their employers. Nevertheless, this does not alter the fact that there is a sense in which wives are called to submit to their husbands in a way that is *nonreciprocal* (see 1 Pet. 3:1–6 in the context of 1 Pet. 2:13, 18). Husbands' exercise of authority, in turn, must not be an arbitrary or abusive one, but should be motivated by love.

Fifth, it must also be pointed out that it is thus manifestly *not* true that wifely submission is *merely a result of the fall*. To the contrary, as mentioned, Genesis 2 contains several indications that headship and submission were part of God's original creation: God created the man first (Gen. 2:7; noted by Paul in 1 Cor. 11:8 and 1 Tim. 2:13) and laid on him a dual charge (Gen. 2:15–17); and God made the woman from the man and for the man (2:21–22; see 1 Cor. 11:8–9) as his suitable helper (Gen. 2:18, 20). God's post-fall judgment in Genesis 3:16 does not alter the fact that male headship is part of the design of the husband-and-wife relationship prior to the fall; it merely addresses the negative consequences of sin on the way in which husband and wife now relate to each other.[23] That wifely submission is not merely a result of the fall is further supported by the present passage, where it is Christian women, that is, those who have been redeemed and regenerated in Christ, who are nonetheless called to submit to their husbands (Eph. 5:22).

Paul rounds out his discussion with a familiar allusion to Scripture: "and the two shall become one flesh" (Eph. 5:31; see Gen. 2:24: "they").[24] Paul's major point seems to be that marriage has the honor of embodying the "one-flesh" principle that later obtained also in the union of the exalted Christ with the church, described by Paul in terms of "head," "members," and "body." Like the inclusion of Gentiles in God's salvific plan, this, too, is a *mystery*: it was hidden in the divine wisdom in ages past but now has been given to Paul to reveal. Marriage is thus shown to be part and parcel of God's overarching purposes of "to bring all things in heaven and on earth together under one head, even Christ" (Eph. 1:10 NIV).

The lesson to be drawn from this is that marriage in Christian teaching, rather than being an end in itself, is subjected to Christ's rule. Just as Christ must rule over all heavenly powers (Eph. 1:21–22) and over the church (Eph. 4:15), he must also rule over the marital relationship (Eph. 5:21–33), the family (Eph. 6:1–4), and the workplace (Eph. 6:5–9). A married couple is part of the church and part of that spiritual warfare that resolutely resists evil (Eph. 6:10–14) and seeks to promote God's purposes in this world (Eph. 6:15, 19–20). Thus the marriage relationship has as an important purpose the bearing of Christian witness in the unbelieving world. Directly, this occurs by the husband's and the wife's living out God's purposes for the Christian couple. Indirectly, this takes place by being part of a biblical church that actively propagates the gospel message.

Not only is marriage therefore part of *God's end-time purposes in Christ* (Eph. 1:10) and part of the *Spirit's operation* (Eph. 5:18), it is also part of one other important larger reality, namely that of *spiritual warfare* (Eph. 6:10–18). Thus marriage ought not to be viewed merely on a horizontal, human plane but should be understood as involving spiritual attacks that require husbands and wives to "put on the full armor of God" in order to withstand those attacks.

PRACTICAL APPLICATION

We note three points of application. First, while some may view submitting to one's husband's authority as something negative, a more accurate way of looking at marital roles is to understand that wives are called to *follow their husband's loving leadership* in their marriage. This leadership and submission is to take place in the context of a true partnership in which the husband genuinely values his wife's companionship and counsel and the wife sincerely esteems her husband's leadership. It is one of the unfortunate legacies of radical feminism that many tend to view male-female relationships in adversarial terms. This is contrary to God's desire and design and to the biblical message.

Second, there is a *difference between traditional and biblical marriage*. Traditional marriage may be understood as the type of division of labor by which women are responsible for cooking, cleaning, doing the laundry, and so on, while men are at work earning the family income. While Scripture does specify work outside the home as men's primary sphere and the home as the center of women's activity (e.g., Gen. 3:16–19; Prov. 31:10–31—though the woman's reach is not *limited* to the home: 1 Tim. 2:15; 5:10, 14), the Bible does not seek to legislate the exact division of labor a husband and wife ought to observe. Hence within the biblical parameters outlined above, there remains room for the individual couple to work out their own distinctive and specific arrangement. This may vary from couple to couple and ought to be considered a part of Christian freedom.

Third and last, *improper caricatures* of the biblical teaching of wifely submission and the husband's loving leadership (which includes the proper exercise of authority) must be *rejected* as either deliberate or unwitting attempts to discredit such a model as unworthy of a woman's human dignity or our modern, "enlightened" times. The kind of submission Scripture is talking about is not akin to *slavery* where one person owns another. It is not *subservience* where one person is doing the bidding of another without intelligent input or interaction. It is not even truly *hierarchical*, since this conjures up notions of a military-style, top-down chain of command in which the soldier is asked to obey, no-questions-asked, the orders of his superior. None of these labels constitutes an accurate description of Scripture with regard to the roles of men and women.

Rather, the biblical model for marriage is that of loving complementarity, where the husband and the wife are partners who value and respect each other and where the husband's loving leadership is met with the wife's intelligent response. If Christ chooses to submit to God the Father while being equal in worth and personhood, there is no good reason why God could not have designed the husband-and-wife relationship in such a way that the wife is called to submit to the man while likewise being equal in worth and personhood. As Paul writes to the Corinthians, "But I want you to understand that the head of every man is Christ, the head of a wife is her husband, and the head of Christ is God" (1 Cor. 11:3).

2

MARRIAGE AND SEX

In this chapter, we will touch on a magnificent yet delicate topic: the ethics of sex. Why did God make man male and female? And what is a proper Christian understanding of sex? The answer to this question is integrally tied to a deeper apprehension of God's plan for the husband and the wife to live life in the way God intended. But before talking about sex, we must briefly discuss an important foundational matter: the nature of marriage. There are three commonly held views: (1) marriage as a sacrament; (2) marriage as a contract; and (3) marriage as a covenant.

THE NATURE OF MARRIAGE
Marriage as a Sacrament
The view of marriage as a sacrament, while harking back to Scripture, is largely a product of church tradition. *Sacramentum* is the Latin term used by Jerome in the fourth-century Vulgate to translate the Greek expression *mystērion* ("mystery"), which, as mentioned, describes the analogy between marriage and the union of Christ and the church in Ephesians 5:32. The *sacramental model* of marriage has its roots in the writings of the influential church father Augustine, who, in his text "On the Good of Marriage," as well as in his later writings, noted three main benefits of marriage: offspring, fidelity, and the sacramental bond.[1] A survey of his works reveals that in using the phrase "sacramental bond" (*sacramentum*) Augustine was trying to communicate that marriage creates a holy, permanent bond between a man and a woman, which depicts Christ's union with the church.

However, as the Roman Catholic Church (which built much of its theology on Augustine's writings) developed its full-fledged sacramental theology including the seven sacraments dispensed by the church, Augustine's concept of marriage was recast. In its reconceived manifestation, officially codified at the Council of Trent (1545–1563), the Roman Catholic Church defined marriage (using Augustinian terminology) as a *sacrament*.[2] According to the sacramental model of marriage, it is by participating in this ecclesiastical rite that grace is accrued for the married couple; this belief is based on the supposition that God dispenses grace through the church and participation in its sacraments.[3] To this end people must approach the sacrament with reverence and faith.

While this view of marriage has proved attractive to some, it is deficient biblically for several reasons.[4] First and foremost, there is nothing in the institution of marriage itself that "mystically" dispenses divine grace.[5] It is not the case, as the Roman Catholic Church maintains, that when marriage is entered into under the auspices of the church, it is in itself an institution where Christ is "personally present" in a mystical way. There is no intrinsic power in the marriage vows themselves. The prerequisite for a Christian marriage is not the "sacramental blessing" of the institutionalized church, but becoming "new creatures" in Christ (see 2 Cor. 5:17; Eph. 4:23–24) by being regenerated, "born again" in him (see Titus 3:5).

Second, this approach to marriage does not cohere with the thrust of the biblical teaching on marriage as a whole, according to which the Creator designed marriage as the vehicle for *creating new physical life*, not as a *mechanism for attaining spiritual life*. In other words, the life imparted through marriage operates through procreation and is extended to a married couple's physical offspring (see Gen. 1:27–28; 2:23–24) rather than being channeled to the couple by virtue of participating in a sacramental or "mystical" ecclesiastical rite in which grace is dispensed by the sheer working of the institution itself.

A third problem with this model of marriage is that it subjects the husband-wife relationship to the control of the church. There is no biblical injunction supporting this notion. Christ himself is said to be the head of the church and the Lord and Savior of both husband and wife (Eph. 5:23–27; see 1 Cor. 11:3). For these and other reasons we conclude that the sacramental model is not borne out by scriptural teaching but is largely a product of patristic and medieval mystical thought that goes beyond and is in fact counter to the biblical conception of marriage. Rightly understood, marriage may be viewed as "sacramental" in the Augustinian sense of constituting a sacred, permanent bond between a man and a woman, but it is not a "sacrament" in the way Roman Catholic theology has defined it.

Marriage as a Contract

A second model of marriage is the *contractual* model. The contractual model constitutes the prevailing secular view of marriage in Western culture.[6] While some have observed that there does not appear to be any major discernible distinction between contracts and covenants in Old Testament times, because people regularly invoked God as a witness when entering into mutual agreements, there is a sharp disjunction between (secular) contracts and (sacred) covenants in modern society.[7]

In contrast to the sacramental model (which at least takes Scripture as its initial point of departure) and the covenantal view (which roots marriage squarely in the biblical teaching on the subject), the contractual approach does not normally invoke Scripture as its grounds of authority. Rather, proponents of this approach view marriage as a bilateral contract that is voluntarily formed, maintained, and dissolved by two individuals. Gary Chapman lists five general characteristics of such contracts:

1. They are typically made for a limited period of time.
2. They most often deal with specific actions.

3. They are conditional upon the continued performance of contractual obligations by the other partner.
4. They are entered into for one's own benefit.
5. They are sometimes unspoken and implicit.[8]

The contractual model, which harkens back to the medieval ecclesiastical courts and the writings of Enlightenment thinkers, roots marriage in civil law.[9] According to this view, the state is charged with overseeing the institution of marriage and has authority to grant both marriage licenses and certificates of divorce. Christians who hold to this model may "Christianize" their marriage by injecting Christian terminology into their vows and by formally commencing their marriage in a church, yet in such cases the officiating minister ultimately only has power to marry couples by the authority vested in him by the state.

Although this is the prevailing model of marriage in Western culture, it has several limitations. First, this teaching is reductionistic. Marriage is an agreement between a man and a woman, but it is much more. In fact, the contractual model did not exist as a developed model of marriage until the seventeenth century at the earliest. It seems unlikely that it would take the church well over a millennium to discover the true nature of marriage.

A second objection is that the contractual model provides an extremely weak basis for the permanence of marriage. In essence, this view bases the security and stability of marriage on people's ability not to sin. If one spouse commits a grievous enough sin to break the contract, the other partner is free to dissolve the union. In light of pervasive human sinfulness, this renders marriage a highly precarious and unstable institution. Scripture, however, stresses the permanence and sacred nature of marriage before God (Matt. 19:4–6, esp. v. 6; see Gen. 2:24).

Third, this model of marriage is inadequate because, by rooting matrimony in civil law, it opens the door (at least in principle) to a variety of marital arrangements that Scripture clearly prohibits. To cite but a few of the more egregious examples, it would only require an amendment of civil law to allow for "legal" same-sex marriage, polygamy, incestuous marriage, bestiality, and so on. Yet Scripture consistently and unequivocally disallows these forms of marriage (e.g., Gen. 1:27–28; 2:23–24; Lev. 18; 20:10–21). For this reason any model of marriage that substitutes human laws for divine revelation as the basis for understanding the nature of this vital relationship falls short of the biblical teaching concerning marriage and should therefore be considered unacceptable for Bible-believing Christians.

None of this is to say that marriages entered into before a public official but not in a church wedding ceremony are invalid or that such couples are not really married. They are. Our point here is simply that those who hold to a contractual view of marriage, while truly married, fall short of what Scripture itself depicts as the nature of the marital bond. If such a couple converts to Christ, therefore, they obviously do not need to get married again, but that couple should commit themselves to a fuller, more adequate understanding of what it means to be married according to Scripture—best described as a covenant.

Marriage as a Covenant

A third approach to the nature of marriage is the covenantal model. This position defines marriage as a sacred bond between a man and a woman instituted by and publicly entered into before God (whether or not this is acknowledged by the married couple), normally consummated by sexual intercourse.[10] Although this view has taken on various nuances in the writings of different authors (and ultimately will be shaped by one's general understanding of biblical covenants), its essence is that marriage is conceived not merely as a bilateral contract between two individuals, but as a sacred bond between husband and wife before God as a witness (see Mal. 2:14).[11]

Unlike the sacramental view, which roots marriage in the standards of *church law* (that is, the church's own understanding of itself and the nature of marriage), and the contractual view, which roots marriage in the standards of *civil law* (that is, human stipulations regulating people's common life in society), the covenantal view roots marriage in the standards of *divine law* (that is, the authoritative divine revelation found in Scripture itself). In keeping with John Stott's definition of marriage on the basis of Genesis 2:24, the covenantal view therefore holds that "marriage is an exclusive heterosexual *covenant between one man and one woman, ordained and sealed by God,* preceded by a public leaving of parents, consummated in sexual union, issuing in a permanent mutually supportive partnership, and normally crowned by the gift of children."[12]

While there are various types of covenants established in Old Testament times, the term *covenant* (Heb. *bᵉrît,* less frequently *'ēšed;* LXX: *diathēkē*) in general conveys "the idea of a solemn commitment, guaranteeing promises or obligations undertaken by one or both covenanting parties."[13] The expression is frequently used for commitments between God and human beings (e.g., the Noahic, Abrahamic, Mosaic, Davidic, and the new covenant), yet it also refers to a variety of agreements between humans (e.g., Gen. 21:22–24; 1 Sam. 18:3; 1 Kings 5:1–12; 2 Kings 11:17), including marriage (Prov. 2:17; Ezek. 16:8; Mal. 2:14). It is therefore important not to import all the features of a divine-human covenant into a given human covenant relationship (such as marriage). For instance, the analogy between marriage and the Christ-church relationship (involving the new covenant) in Ephesians 5:21–33 should not be taken to imply that these are equivalent in every respect. The new covenant, for its part, is eternal, while marriage, according to Jesus, is limited to this life only (Matt. 22:30).

In addition, it should be recognized that the biblical notion of marriage as a covenant at the very least incorporates contractual features. As Instone-Brewer points out, the Hebrew word (*bᵉrît*) is the same for both contract and covenant, and the theological meaning of *covenant* is "an agreement that a faithful person would not break even if the partner to whom that person is in covenant breaks the stipulations of the covenant."[14] The later prophets (esp. Jeremiah 31; see Ezekiel 36–37), however, spoke of a "new covenant" that God would promise to keep whether or not his people would. According to Instone-Brewer, this irrevocable covenant is unlike any other Old Testament covenant, and it is the irrevocable nature of the new covenant that makes it so special and unique.

Advocates of the covenantal model of marriage support this view primarily with reference to two clusters of passages: (1) covenantal language in the Genesis 2 narrative recounting the divine institution of marriage between the first man and the first woman; and (2) passages of Scripture that explicitly refer to marriage as a "covenant," as well as biblical analogies and passages in which marriage is implicitly treated in covenantal terms.[15]

Covenantal language in the foundational Genesis narrative may include the reference to the "one flesh" union between husband and wife in Genesis 2:24. The consummation of marriage through sexual intercourse may serve as the equivalent to the oath in other Old Testament covenants.[16] Adam's naming of Eve in Genesis 2:23 is consistent with God's changing the names of Abram and Jacob upon entering into a covenant relationship with them (Gen. 17:5; 35:10).

Explicit biblical terminology referring to marriage as a "covenant" includes the reference to the adulterous woman forgetting "the covenant of her God" in Proverbs 2:16–17. This most likely refers to the (written or oral) marriage agreement between the woman and her husband before God,[17] as is suggested by a similar reference in the book of Malachi: "The LORD was witness between you and the wife of your youth, . . . your companion and your wife by *covenant*" (*bᵉrit*; Mal. 2:14; see Ezek. 16:8).[18]

Implications of a Covenant View of Marriage

In light of the above observations, what does it mean for a couple to embrace the view of marriage as a covenant? If the marriage covenant is defined as *a sacred bond instituted by and publicly entered into before God (whether or not this is acknowledged by the married couple), normally consummated by sexual intercourse*, embracing the "marriage covenant" concept means a couple must understand and commit itself to at least the following five things:

1. *The permanence of marriage.* Marriage is intended to be permanent, since it was established by God (Matt. 19:6; Mark 10:9). Marriage constitutes a serious commitment that should not be entered into lightly or unadvisedly. It involves a solemn promise or pledge, not merely to one's marriage partner, but before God. Divorce is not permitted except perhaps in certain biblically prescribed circumstances.

2. *The sacredness of marriage.* Marriage is not merely a human agreement between two consenting individuals (a "civil union"); it is a relationship before and under God (Gen. 2:22). Hence, a "same-sex" marriage is an oxymoron; since Scripture universally condemns homosexual relationships, God would never sanction a sacred marital bond between two members of the same sex. While sacred, however, marriage is not therefore a "sacrament."

3. *The intimacy of marriage.* Marriage is the most intimate of all human relationships, uniting a man and a woman in a "one flesh" bond (Gen. 2:23–25). Marriage involves "leaving" one's family of origin and "being united" to one's spouse, which signifies the establishment of a new family unit distinct from the two originating families. While "one flesh" suggests sexual intercourse and normally procreation, at its very heart the concept entails the establishment of a new kinship relation between two previously unrelated individuals by the most intimate of human bonds.

4. *The mutuality of marriage.* Marriage is a relationship of free self-giving of one human being to another (Eph. 5:25–30). The marriage partners are to be first and foremost concerned about the well-being of the other person and to be committed to each other in steadfast love and devotion. "Mutuality," however, does not mean "sameness in role." Scripture is clear that

wives are to submit to their husbands and to be their "suit-able helpers," while husbands bear the ultimate responsibil-ity for the marriage before God (Eph. 5:22–24; Col. 3:18; see Gen. 2:18, 20).

5. *The exclusiveness of marriage.* Marriage is not only permanent, sacred, intimate, and mutual; it is also exclusive (Gen. 2:22–25; 1 Cor. 7:2–5). This means that no other human relationship must interfere with the marriage commitment between husband and wife. For this reason our Lord treated sexual immorality of a married person (Matt. 19:9; including even a husband's lustful thoughts, Matt. 5:28) with utmost seriousness. For this reason, too, premarital sex is illegitimate, since it violates the exclusive claims of one's future spouse.

SEX

The "What" and the "Why" of Sex

In most cases, even for Christians, the "what" of sex garners the lion's share of attention,[19] while the "why" of sex is regularly neglected.[20] As a result, there is no lack of non-Christian, and Christian, resources on sex, and how to have better sex, while there is a relative dearth on conscious Christian reflection on the deeper meaning of and purpose for sex. Yet this lack of proper theological grounding comes at a cost: the loss of a more profound, heartfelt union between those engaging in sex, including Christian couples. As Geoffrey Bromiley maintains in *God and Marriage*:

> Far too many people, Christians not excluded, are self-cen-teredly preoccupied with their own marital problems and their attempts to engineer solutions to them. A theology of marriage can help them to achieve a God-centered look at the larger situation of which their marriages constitute a small, if by no means unimportant, part. In the long run, a new look means a new understanding, and a new understanding means a new practice.[21]

The same is true regarding a theology of sex. Sex is such an important part of our lives that it seems appropriate for us as Christians to reflect theologically on this vital subject, not merely because, like any other area of our lives, we want to submit our sexual practice to the lordship of Christ, but because we want to understand God's purpose for sex—for his greater glory and for our own good.

The Purposes of Sex

What is the purpose and deeper meaning of sex? The world's answer is that sex exists for one's pleasure and fulfillment. Yet while sex is a vital part of human existence, it is a gift of God not to be idolized, and the belief that sex, or love, can "save" a person, while powerful and persistent, is only a myth. As Scripture makes clear, *God* is love (1 John 4:8), but love is not God. In fact, when made the object of worship, sex turns into an idol and becomes the sure victim of unrealistically high expectations.[22]

The Bible teaches that sex is part of one's calling to live life to the glory of God. Thus sex, like all aspects of our lives, is to be placed "in the service of God."[23] For this reason the purpose of sex transcends the individual couple and the fulfillment of self; it is rooted in the heart and creative purposes of God and therefore should be oriented toward him. As we have seen, marriage is not merely a human convention but a divine institution, and God's plan for marriage is that of a faithful, lifelong covenant relationship characterized by permanence, sacredness, intimacy, mutuality, and exclusiveness. Submitted to God, and in keeping with his creative purposes, marriage, including sex, is thus the vehicle by which God is glorified and the marriage partners experience the growing fulfillment that comes from living their lives the way their good, faithful, and loving Creator intended them to be lived.

In the first and subsequent centuries of the Christian era, the belief gained ground that those who would be pure and holy and spiritual before God should refrain from sex altogether and remain in a state of celibacy or, if already married, continence.[24] The cult of virginity became widespread in Christendom, and those who were spiritually zealous and sincere frequently entered the monastic orders and withdrew in order to spend their days in quiet contemplation and solitude.[25] As we have seen, however, the Old Testament joyfully affirms the beauty of sex in marriage, and the New Testament likewise extols the goodness of everything that God created, including sex, as long as it is enjoyed within the parameters established by the Creator.

Sex, therefore, is God's good gift to a husband and wife and is to be enjoyed in keeping with his purposes. So what are the divinely ordained purposes for sex? The first purpose is *procreational*. After God made humanity male and female, he said to them, "Be fruitful and multiply and fill the earth and subdue it" (Gen. 1:28; see Gen. 9:1). Thus procreation is part of God's creation mandate for the man and the woman. Procreation is also the natural outflow of sexual union unless hindered by contraceptive devices, thwarted by abortion, or prevented by infertility. Procreation ensures the continuation of the human race and enables it to fulfill God's mandate of cultivating the earth for God. Thus sex, leading to procreation, fulfills an indispensable function in God's plan for humanity. It is in a true sense "sex in the service of God."

The second purpose for sex is tied to the *relational* and *social* dimension of the husband-wife relationship.[26] When God created the woman, he declared, "It is not good that the man should be alone; I will make him a helper fit for him" (Gen. 2:18). God proceeded to fashion a woman from one of the man's ribs and brought her to the man who exclaimed, "This at last is bone of my bones and flesh of my flesh; she shall be called Woman, because she was taken out of Man" (Gen. 2:21–23). Thus the male-female relationship, including its sexual component, serves also the purpose of alleviating the man's aloneness and of providing companionship, resulting in the man and the woman becoming "one flesh" (Gen. 2:24).

Third is what Christopher Ash calls "the *public good*." According to Ash, this public good

> encompasses the benefits of ordered and regulated sexual relationships in human society. Undisciplined and disordered sexual behavior must be restrained, for it carries with it a high social and personal cost in family breakdown, destructive jealousies, resentments, bitterness and hurt. Ordered behavior is to be encouraged because this has benefits that extend beyond the couple to children, neighbours and the wider networks of relational society.[27]

In conjunction with the public dimension of marriage, public restraint is necessary for at least three reasons.[28] The first is fallen man's tendency to pursue the fulfillment of his sexual desires in a disorderly, at times even random, fashion. Men, in particular, often find it difficult to control their thoughts and actions in this area and, unless publicly restrained, may commit acts of sexual impropriety. Second, public restraint is needed because of the reality of sexual arousal. The Old Testament repeatedly warns against the uncovering of nakedness (e.g., Ezek. 16:36; 23:18). This calls for modesty on the part of women and public constraints regarding the display of nudity. Third, there is a need for sexual intercourse to be ordered to the right ends, which has important ramifications for the proscription of prostitution.[29]

Last but not least, sex, especially when enjoyed between a husband and a wife in the context of a faithful, lifelong marital union, gives great *pleasure*. Sexual stimulation, the sexual climax, and sexual fulfillment are God's gracious gift for humanity, to be gratefully enjoyed without shame, guilt, or fear. Within the marriage bond, sex becomes the ultimate physical expression of deep, committed, and devoted love.

PRACTICAL IMPLICATIONS

In monogamous marriage, a husband and a wife have the wonderful privilege to "become one flesh" and to be "naked and not ashamed" (Gen. 2:24–25). Sex is one of our Creator's most wonderful, exhilarating gifts, and one that is to be enjoyed in a context of Christian freedom and love. The question arises, however: Are there any boundaries for sex that mark what is or is not acceptable based on a Christian theology of sex and general biblical morality? There are at least ten things that are not acceptable for Christian sexual activity according to Scripture: (1) fornication; (2) adultery; (3) homosexuality; (4) impurity; (5) orgies; (6) prostitution; (7) lust; (8) sodomy; (9) incest; and (10) obscenity and inappropriate sexual language.

Beyond this, the following general principles will serve as helpful guidelines as a husband and wife consider what is or is not acceptable to God with regard to sexual activity.[30] (1) Is a given sexual practice or activity prohibited in Scripture or does it violate scriptural moral principles? If not, this may be a matter in which Christians have freedom of discretion (1 Cor. 6:12). (2) Is a given sexual practice or activity beneficial or harmful physically, emotionally, and/or spiritually? If harmful, it should be avoided (1 Cor. 6:12). (3) Does a given sexual practice or activity involve persons outside the marriage relationship? If so, or if a practice becomes public, it is wrong, because Scripture commands those who are married to keep the marriage bed undefiled (Heb. 13:4).

3

FAMILY IN
THE BIBLE

What is a family? Building on our definition of marriage in the previous chapter, we may define family as, primarily, one man and one woman united in matrimony (barring death of a spouse) plus (normally) natural or adopted children and, secondarily, any other persons related by blood.[1] In biblical times, extended families lived together in larger households, while in modern Western culture the family unit is usually comprised of the nuclear family (father, mother, and children) living in the same household.[2] In the following survey, we will investigate the ancient Israelite conception of family and explore the teaching on the roles and responsibilities of fathers, mothers, and children in both Testaments.

FAMILY IN THE OLD TESTAMENT
The Ancient Israelite Conception of Family
Because of their descent from a common ancestor, the Israelites perceived themselves as a large extended kinship group.[3] The Old Testament features four major Hebrew terms related to family, translated in English as *people*, *tribe*, *clan*, and *house of a father*. While "people" typically refers to the nation of Israel and "tribe" reflects the people's tribal structure as descendants of the twelve sons of Jacob, "clan" usually designates a subgroup smaller than the tribe but larger than the family.

The most relevant Hebrew expression for our present purposes is the fourth one—"house of a father," which could also be translated "family" (lit., "father's house"; see, e.g., Judges 17–18). Unlike the modern Western notion of a nuclear family consisting of husband, wife, and children, ancient Israelite households were comprised of large extended families, which could include a couple's married children's families, any as of yet unmarried sons and daughters, and male and female hired servants and slaves along with their families.

The Role and Responsibilities of Fathers

While most identify the ancient Israelite family structure by the term "patriarchy" ("rule of the father"), "patricentrism" ("centered around the father") may be better suited for this type of arrangement, since, first, feminism has permanently discredited patriarchy even in its nonabusive forms by giving it a negative connotation, and, second, "patricentrism" better reflects the "normative biblical disposition toward the role of the head of a household in Israel."[4] Like the spokes of a wheel, family life radiated outward from the father as its center. The community was built around the father and bore his stamp in every respect. Also, third, while the father indisputably ruled his household, the Old Testament rarely focuses on his power (Gen. 3:16 speaks of a subversion of the man's proper exercise of authority). Rather than functioning as a despot or dictator, in healthy households the father and husband usually inspired the trust and security of its members (see Job 29:12–17; Ps. 68:5–6). Therefore, it was not primarily the power and privileges associated with the father's position but rather the responsibilities associated with his headship that were emphasized.

Daniel Block lists the following nine primary responsibilities of the father in ancient Israel:[5]

- modeling strict personal fidelity to Yahweh;
- leading the family in the national festivals, nurturing the memory of Israel's salvation;

- instructing the family in the traditions of the exodus and the Scriptures (Deut. 6:4–9, 20–25; 11:18–25);
- managing the land in accordance with the Law (Leviticus 25);
- providing for the family's basic needs for food, shelter, clothing, and rest;
- defending the household against outside threats (e.g., Judg. 18:21–25);
- serving as elder and representing the household in the official assembly of citizens (Ruth 4:1–11);
- maintaining family members' well-being and the harmonious operation of the family unit; and
- implementing decisions made at the clan or tribal level.

Apart from their responsibilities toward their wife (or wives), fathers also had obligations toward their children. The following list demonstrates the inadequacy of labeling the father's role in ancient Israel "patriarchal" with the predominant or even exclusive emphasis being placed on his exercise (or even abusive exercise) of authority. Fathers' responsibilities toward their sons included the following:[6]

- naming their children (together with their wives) (e.g., Gen. 16:15; 17:19);
- consecrating their firstborn sons to God (see Ex. 13:2, 12–15; 22:29; 34:1–20);
- circumcising their sons on the eighth day (Gen. 17:12; 21:4; Lev. 12:3);
- delighting in, having compassion on, and loving their sons (e.g., Ps. 103:13);
- nurturing their sons' spiritual development, modeling before them their own deep personal commitment to God and the Scriptures, instructing them in the Scriptures and the traditions of salvation and covenant, and giving public witness to their spiritual commitment (see Ex. 12:24; 13:8);
- guarding their own ethical conduct so as not to involve their sons in their sin (Ex. 20:5; Deut. 5:9);
- instructing their sons in the way of wisdom, developing their

character and skills for life and vocation and teaching them to follow in their father's steps (Proverbs 1–9);

- disciplining their sons when they erred and presenting them to the communal leaders for discipline when the sons refused to be corrected (see Deut. 8:5; 2 Sam. 7:14);
- judiciously managing their household affairs, especially with regard to inheritance, so as to ensure a smooth transition to the subsequent generation;
- arranging for their sons' marriage to suitable wives (Genesis 24; Judges 14);
- pronouncing blessings on their sons prior to their death (Genesis 27; 48–49).

The list of a father's obligations toward his daughters is shorter, given the generally male-oriented perspective of the Old Testament:

- protecting his daughters from male "predators" so they would marry as virgins, thus bringing honor to his name and purity to their husbands (see Ex. 22:16–17; Deut. 22:13–21);
- arranging for his daughters' marriages by finding suitable husbands and making proper arrangements;
- ensuring a measure of security for his daughters by providing a dowry (see Gen. 29:24, 29);
- protecting his daughters from rash vows (Num. 30:2–15);
- providing security for his daughters in case their marriages failed; and perhaps also
- instructing his daughters in the Scriptures.

The Role and Responsibilities of Mothers

The Old Testament contains many indications of an elevated status of the wife and mother in ancient Israel. (1) In Genesis 1 and 2, the woman, like the man, was created by God in his likeness (Gen. 1:27); (2) the man and the woman are to have joint responsibility for subduing the earth and cultivating it (Gen. 1:28); (3) the woman is placed alongside the man as his "suitable helper," not as his servant or slave (Gen. 2:18, 20); (4) the woman's creation from the man's rib may also convey the notion that she is close and dear to his heart (Gen. 2:22); (5) the woman's name in the Hebrew designates her as the man's counterpart (Gen. 2:23); and (6) the one-flesh union between husband and wife also accentuates their closeness and intimacy (Gen. 2:24–25). At the same time, it is clear that the wife and mother was functionally subordinated to her husband and male head of the household.

The following list bears testimony to the dignity of the wife and mother and her influence within the household in ancient Israel:[7]

- men and women related to each other on a complementary level both in courtship and, once married, in lovemaking (Song of Solomon);
- wives and mothers often named their children (e.g., Gen. 29:32; 30:6; 35:18; 38:29);
- the fifth commandment stipulates that children honor their fathers *and mothers* (Ex. 20:12; Deut. 5:16);
- both father and mother rose to their daughters' defense if their virginity at the time of her wedding was called into question;
- Old Testament Wisdom Literature often sets a mother's wisdom in instruction in parallelism to that of a father (Prov. 1:8; 6:20);
- the excellent wife in Proverbs 31 exudes initiative, creativity, and energy; while subordinate to her husband, she is not subservient to him;
- women often exercised great influence over their husbands, both positive and negative;
- although excluded from official leadership roles in the community, they were occasionally appointed in ad hoc prophetic roles and participated in religious affairs.

Proverbs 31 summarizes the mother's responsibilities to her children: providing food, clothing, and shelter. At a child's birth, mothers would cut the umbilical cord, bathe the child, and wrap it in a cloth (see Ezek. 16:3–4). During the first decade of the child's life, he or she was the special concern of his or her mother. Since in ancient Israel the home was the primary place for education, the mother's example and instruction were vital. Once children reached adolescence, they would increasingly spend more time with their fathers, though this does not mean that the mothers' influence was no longer felt. Mothers would also train their daughters for their future roles as wives and mothers. This was even more important since daughters upon marriage would leave their paternal household and join that of their husband. Nevertheless, mothers would continue to follow the course of their daughters' lives, and being able to witness the birth of grandchildren was considered to be a special blessing and delight (e.g., Ruth 4:14–16). Mothers also bore responsibilities toward domestic servants and slaves.[8]

The Role and Responsibilities of Children

The most common Hebrew terms for children in the Old Testament are translated in English as *son, daughter, fetus, male child* or *youth, female child*, and *seed*. The Hebrew Scriptures also feature a considerable variety of terms for the different stages of childhood (including words for unborn children, newborns, infants, and nursing and weaned children) and young adulthood (including terms for adolescents as well as young women of childbearing age and young men, the latter especially in the book of Proverbs). Childhood was considered to extend from one month to five years and youth from five to twenty years (Lev. 27:1–7).

The esteem in which children were held in ancient Israel (which is reflected in the breadth of vocabulary used for children and youth) can be attributed to several factors and convictions:[9] (1) the belief that every human being is created in the image of God (Gen. 1:27; Psalm 8); (2) the view that children ensure the perpetuation of humanity and the fulfillment of the divine mandate to subdue and cultivate the earth (Gen. 1:26; 5; 9:18–19); (3) the notion that the conception of children was ultimately a product of divine action and hence a sign of God's favor (with the corollary that barrenness was viewed as a sign of divine disfavor); (4) the valuing of children as an important economic asset; (5) the belief that in a sense parents live on in and through their children (hence one's worst fate was for one's "seed" to be cut off and one's "name" to be blotted out; see 1 Sam. 24:21; 2 Sam. 14:7; Ps. 37:28; Isa. 14:20–21).

The firstborn was held in particularly high esteem as the privileged heir. Firstborn sons were acknowledged as belonging to God and consecrated to him in a special ceremony. Circumcision was another exceedingly important religious rite, serving as a mark of the covenant. It was carried out on male infants on the eighth day after birth (Genesis 17). Otherwise, there were no uniform ceremonies to mark events in the lives of young people in ancient Israel. The book of Proverbs provides a fascinating glimpse into the training of young men in wisdom and discretion.

Expectations and responsibilities for children in ancient Israel varied depending on age. The first and foremost responsibility of children and young people, however, was respect for parents. This expectation was made explicit in numerous ways, not least in its position as the first of the horizontal covenant principles mentioned in the Ten Commandments (Ex. 20:12; Deut. 5:16). Second, when old enough, children were expected to help in and around the parental home in a variety of ways including such things as harvesting, hunting, and caregiving.[10] Beyond this, adult children were expected, if necessary, to guard the genealogical integrity of a family through "levirate marriage," a marriage between a widow whose husband had died without having left a male offspring and the brother of the deceased (i.e., the brother of a deceased man was expected to marry the widow; Deut. 25:5–10). In addition, children were responsible to provide for their parents in their old age, which is one reason why childlessness caused considerable anxiety.

The Importance of Teaching Children about God
Passing on the Message

Prior to entering the Promised Land, the Israelites were reminded of God's revelation to them after they had left Egypt and had embarked on their exodus. This reminder encompassed the law (Deut. 4:1–14, esp. v. 9), including the Ten Commandments (Deut. 5:6–21); the Shema ("Hear, O Israel: The LORD our God, the LORD is one" Deut. 6:4); and the greatest commandment: "You shall love the LORD your God with all your heart and with all your soul and with all your might" (Deut. 6:5). Then the Israelites were given the following charge: "And these words that I command you today shall be on your heart. You shall teach them diligently to your children, and shall talk of them when you sit in your house, and when you walk by the way, and when you lie down, and when you rise" (Deut. 6:6–7; see Deut. 4:9).

Once in the Promised Land, the Israelites were not to forget the Lord who had delivered them from bondage in Egypt. They were to diligently keep his commandments and "do what is right and good in the sight of the LORD, that it may go well with" them (Deut. 6:18). Moreover, "When your son asks you in time to come, 'What is the meaning of the testimonies and the statutes and the rules that the LORD our God has commanded you?'" the Israelites were to testify to God's deliverance and revelation (Deut. 6:20–25). This echoes Moses's earlier instruction subsequent to the institution of the Passover during the exodus where the Israelites are told to impart the message of God's deliverance of the nation to their offspring (Ex. 13:14).

After crossing the Red Sea, Joshua is similarly concerned that the significance of God's redemptive acts is passed on to succeeding generations: "When your children ask in time to come, 'What do those stones mean to you?' then you shall tell them that the waters of the Jordan were cut off before the ark of the covenant of the LORD. When it passed over the Jordan, the waters of the Jordan were cut off. So these stones shall be to the people of Israel a memorial forever" (Josh. 4:6–7; see 4:21–22).

The psalmist, too, underscores the importance of teaching one's children about God. He pledges that he will not hide what God has done in ages past from his children "but tell to the coming generation the glorious deeds of the LORD, and his might, and the wonders that he has done" (Ps. 78:4). He will speak to them about the law, which God "commanded our fathers to teach to their children, that the next generation might know them, the children yet unborn, and arise and tell them to their children, so that they should set their hope in God and not forget the works of God, but keep his commandments; and that they should not be like their fathers, a stubborn and rebellious generation" (Ps. 78:5–8). Thus, from generation to generation, God's ways and will are to be passed on for children to learn from the sins of their fathers and for God to be known as mighty and glorious.

The five books of Moses, the Old Testament historical books, and the book of Psalms are pervaded by the consciousness that parents (and especially fathers) must pass on their religious heritage to their children. God's express will for his people Israel is still his will for God's people in the church today. Christian parents have the mandate and serious obligation to instill their religious heritage to their children. This heritage centers on the personal experience of God's deliverance from sin and his revelation in the Lord Jesus Christ and his death for us on the cross. Christian parents ought to take every opportunity to speak about these all-important matters with their children and to express and impart to their children personal gratitude for what God has done for their children. While there may be Christian Sunday school teachers and other significant people in a child's life, parents must never neglect their God-given responsibility to be the primary source of religious instruction for their children.

Training up a Child

The book of Proverbs' teaching on childrearing is perhaps best encapsulated by the familiar verse, "Train up a child in the way he should go; even when he is old he will not depart from it" (Prov. 22:6). While this is not a divine promise, it is the product of keen and solid observation of what usually occurs in life, and this should be taken seriously. In the end, however, children do make their own decision as to which way they want to go. Most likely, once grown, children tend to follow in the path they were shown when still a child. This is why parental discipline and instruction are so important and why obedience and respect for authority must be infused in a child during his or her formative years.

According to the book of Proverbs, the *purpose* of biblical parental instruction is to *inculcate wisdom and the fear of the Lord* (which is the beginning of wisdom, 1:7) into sons and daughters.[11] Wise children bring great gladness and joy to parents (23:24–25; 29:3, 17), while foolish ones bring grief (10:1), shame (28:7), and, in some cases, ruin to parents (19:13). Essentially, young people must choose between two ways: the way of wisdom or the way of folly. By their very nature, children are *simple* and in need of instruction (1:22). They lack sense and are naïve and gullible (14:15), which makes them vulnerable to wrong influences if not trained in character (9:16). Unless corrected, what starts out as naïve simplicity leads to full-grown folly (14:18), which can be avoided through proper instruction in biblical wisdom.

The value of wisdom is manifold, and to instruct children in this wisdom is life-giving. Wisdom rescues young men from the wiles of the adulteress (2:16–19; 5; 6:20–35; 7; 22:14; 23:26–28; 31:3). Wisdom also leads young people to submit to parental discipline and correction (3:11–12 [quoted in Heb. 12:5–6]; 15:32; 23:13–14). In fact, wisdom, which is part of the very fabric of creation (8:22–31), is their very life (4:13), that is, wisdom is not merely a state of mind but provides real protection from danger or even death. Essentially, what young people must be taught by their parents, is to trust the Lord with all their heart and to acknowledge him in all their ways, rather than being self-reliant or following the wrong kinds of role models or influences (3:5–6).

By example and explicit instruction, parents are to teach their children and youth a wide array of positive attributes:[12]

- Diligence and industriousness (6:6–11; 11:27; 12:24; 13:4; 15:19; 18:9; 19:24; 20:4, 13; 21:5; 22:13; 26:13–16)
- Justice (11:1; 16:11; 17:23; 20:10, 23; 31:8–9)
- Kindness (11:17)
- Generosity (11:24; 19:6)
- Self-control, particularly of speech (12:18; 13:3; 21:23) and temper (14:17, 29; 15:18; 16:32; 19:11; see also 25:28)
- Righteousness (12:21, 28; 14:34)
- Truthfulness and honesty (12:22; 16:13; 24:26)
- Discretion in choosing friends (13:20; 18:24), particularly a spouse (18:22; 31:10–31)
- Caution and prudence (14:16; 27:12)
- Gentleness (15:1, 4)
- Contentment (15:16–17; 16:8; 17:1)
- Integrity of character (15:27; 28:18)
- Humility (16:19; 18:12; 22:4)
- Graciousness (16:24)
- Forthrightness (16:30; 17:20)
- Restraint (17:14, 27–28; 18:6–7; 29:20)
- Faithfulness in friendship (17:17) and otherwise (28:20)
- Purity (20:9; 22:11)
- Vigorous pursuit of what is good and right (20:29)
- Skillfulness in work (22:29)
- Patience (25:15)

Negatively, parents are to teach their children to refrain from a pleasure-seeking lifestyle (21:17), particularly from engaging in partying and gluttonous eating and drinking (23:20–21; 28:7). Children and youth should be taught not to be arrogant or vain (21:24). To this end, parents are to administer proper *discipline*, to which children ought to submit: "My son, do not despise the Lord's discipline or be weary of his reproof, for the Lord reproves him whom he loves, as a father the son in whom he delights" (3:11–12; see 13:1). This includes physical discipline: "Whoever spares the rod hates his son, but he who loves him is diligent to discipline him" (13:24; see 22:15; 23:13–14). If a child is left to his or her own devices, the only predictable result is shame (29:15). Although some today find physical discipline troubling, the inspired biblical book of Proverbs presents discipline (including physical discipline) as part of wisdom, and thus the appropriate use of it should not be ruled out for Christian parents today.[13]

FAMILY IN THE NEW TESTAMENT
The Example and Teaching of Jesus
First-Century Palestine and Jesus's Example

In Jesus's day, the extended family lived together (e.g., Mark 1:30), typically sharing a three- or four-room home. Like their mothers, daughters were to take a domestic role, and boys were to emulate their father's example according to the ancient Israelite maxim "like father, like son."[14] Jesus himself learned his father's trade as a craftsman (Matt. 13:55; Mark 6:3). A variety of Geek terms used in the New Testament refer to children, translated in English as *baby, infant, fetus; small child* (three or four years of age); *child* (offspring in general); *small child* (normally below age of puberty); *young person* (normally below age of puberty). This indicates an awareness of the child in its social setting and stages of development. Jesus himself modeled obedience in relation to his earthly parents (Luke 2:51) and supremely toward his heavenly Father (e.g., Mark 14:36; see Heb. 5:8).

Jesus's Teaching on the Family and Discipleship

While Jesus affirmed marriage and blessed children, he conceived of the community of believers in familial terms transcending those of people's natural relations. This is one of the most striking, distinctive, and central aspects of Jesus's call to discipleship. In Jesus's own words, "If anyone comes to me and does not hate his own father and mother and wife and children and brothers and sisters, yes, and even his own life, he cannot be my disciple."[15] In keeping with Old Testament prediction, Jesus came not to bring peace but a sword, "to set a man against his father, and a daughter against her mother, and a daughter-in-law against her mother-in-law. And a person's enemies will be those of his own household" (Matt. 10:34–36).

In his personal experience, Jesus knew spiritual rejection even within his natural family (Mark 3:21; 6:1–6a; John 7:1–9) and asserted that his primary loyalty and that of his followers must be to God the Father (Luke 2:49; Mark 3:31–35). Leaving one's natural family behind, even literally, was regularly expected of Jesus's first followers, at least for the duration of Jesus's three-year earthly ministry (though it appears that subsequently the disciples resumed normal family relations, 1 Cor. 9:5). This is made clear by what is perhaps the earliest account of Jesus's calling of his disciples in Mark's Gospel, where Jesus calls Simon, Simon's brother Andrew, and the sons of Zebedee, and these fishermen leave their natural vocation and family contexts in order to follow Jesus (Mark 1:16–20 = Matt. 4:18–22; see Luke 5:2–11). Those who resist Jesus's call to discipleship are frequently unwilling to forsake their natural ties in favor of total allegiance to Jesus (Luke 9:58, 60, 62; see Matt. 8:19–22).

The Gospels also record a rich young man's unwillingness to part with his wealth in order to follow Jesus, setting his refusal in contrast to the disciples' unconditional commitment to their Master (Mark 10:17–31 = Matt. 19:16–30 = Luke 18:18–30). Upon Peter's remark that he and his fellow disciples have left everything to follow him, Jesus responds with the promise that there is "no one who has left house or brothers or sisters or mother or father or children or lands, for my sake and for the gospel, who will not receive a hundredfold now in this time, houses and brothers and sisters and mothers and children and lands, with persecutions, and in the age to come eternal life" (Mark 10:29–31 and parallels).

Jesus himself set the example by repeatedly renouncing his own natural family ties where they potentially stood in conflict with higher spiritual loyalties. Thus, the twelve-year-old Jesus responded to his parents' anguished concern: "Why were you looking for me? Did you not know that I must be in my Father's house?" (Luke 2:49). Later, Jesus rebukes first his mother and then his brothers for failing to understand the divine timing underlying his ministry (John 2:4; 7:6–8). At another occasion, he refused to be drawn back into the confines of his natural relations when his concerned family went to take charge of him, affirming that, "Whoever does the will of God, he is my brother and sister and mother" (Mark 3:31–35; see 3:20–21). In due course, it appears that Jesus's mother and (at least some of) his brothers acknowledged that they, too, must subordinate their familial claims to Jesus as their Savior and Lord (e.g., Acts 1:14; see Luke 1:46–47).

Examples could be multiplied (e.g., Luke 11:27–28; John 19:26–27), but the implications of Jesus's teaching on discipleship are clear. Rather than preaching a gospel urging believers to make marriage and family their ultimate priority—though obviously these have a vital place in God's purposes for humanity—Jesus placed natural kinship ties in the larger context of the kingdom of God. Thus, while Jesus affirmed natural relations, such as the divine institution of marriage and the need to honor one's parents (Mark 10:8–9, 19), he acknowledged the higher calling of discipleship. One's commitment to truth may lead to division, not peace, in one's natural family (Matt. 10:34), and in this case following Jesus must take precedence.[16]

While Jesus placed people's obligations within the larger framework of God's kingdom, however, this does not imply that Christians are to neglect their family responsibilities. As Paul would later write, "But if anyone does not provide for his relatives, and especially for members of his household, he has denied the faith and is worse than an unbeliever" (1 Tim. 5:8). Clearly, Jesus's physical presence on this earth and his three-year public ministry necessitated unconditional physical following of the Master in a unique way. At the same time, the spiritual principle that following Jesus ought to be every Christian's first priority continues to apply, and where this brings an individual into conflict with his or her natural family obligations, he or she must first seek God's kingdom and his righteousness (Matt. 6:33).

Children in the Ministry of Jesus

Jesus did not deal with children merely on the level of what they should do or think but on the level of who they were in God's eyes. Studying how Jesus understood children can help us know how we should view and relate to our own and others' children. Jesus's earthly ministry intersected with children on a number of occasions. Jesus more than once *restored children to their parents by way of miraculous healing.*[17] In one instance, Jesus put a child in the disciples' midst as an example of the *nature of discipleship,* asserting that, "Whoever receives one such child in my name receives me, and whoever receives me, receives not me but him who sent me" (Mark 9:36–37 and parallels). This must have been startling for Jesus's audience, since in his day it would have been uncommon for adults to think they could learn anything from a child. At another juncture, children were brought to Jesus to receive a blessing from him (Mark 10:13–16 and parallels).

The climactic pronouncement, "I tell you the truth, anyone who will not receive the kingdom of God like a little child will never enter it" (Mark 10:15 NIV), ties together the earlier-recorded instances of Jesus's receptivity toward children with an important characteristic of the kingdom, a humble lack of regard for one's own supposed status (see Luke 22:26). For Jesus, there is no better way to illustrate God's free, unmerited grace than pointing to a child.[18] For, unlike many adults, children are generally entirely unpretentious about receiving a gift. Moreover, "little ones," that is, the least regardless of age, are a repeated focus in Jesus's teaching on discipleship (Matt. 18:5; Luke 9:48). God's kingdom must be entered in a childlike spirit, a lesson that was yet to be learned by Jesus's followers.

In sayings preserved by Matthew, Jesus focuses even more specifically on the sense of dependency and trust that are characteristic of children and that are traits essential for those who would enter his kingdom. In Matthew 11:25–26, Jesus praises the Father for concealing his truth from the self-proclaimed wise and understanding and revealing it to little children. This statement turns out to be prophetic when in Matthew 21:15 the children are shouting in the temple, "Hosanna to the Son of David!" while the chief priests and the teachers of the law are indignant at the sight of the children's praise of Jesus and of "the wonderful things that he did."

According to Jesus, the quality in children that is most emblematic of kingdom virtues is their *low status*. Unless an individual therefore turns and becomes like a child, he will never enter the kingdom of heaven (Matt. 18:3). While children may not necessarily be humble in a spiritual sense—much less "innocent"—their lack of status, their unpretentiousness, and their dependence on others make them suitable illustrations of the need for would-be candidates for Jesus's kingdom to become nothing and be stripped of their earthly status (see Phil. 2:6–7). Hence they embody Jesus's radical call for discipleship and his requirement for his followers to "take up their cross" in total self-abandonment (e.g., Mark 8:34–38 and parallels).

Overall, then, we learn from Jesus that we should not look down on children because they are not fully grown and hence are of lower social status than adults. Like Jesus, we should treat children with respect and dignity, as unique and precious creatures made by God and valuable in his sight. What is more, contrary to our natural inclination that may tell us that we can learn nothing from children and that the relationship is strictly one-way from parent or adult to child, we should look at children also from the vantage point of desirable kingdom traits they may exemplify in a more pronounced way than we do ourselves. This is one way in which God defies the wisdom of those who are wise in their own eyes and the pride of those who think they are something in and of themselves (Matt. 11:25–27; see 1 Cor. 1:27–29).

Paul's Teaching on the Role of Fathers, Mothers, and Children
The Ancient Household and "Household Codes"

Unlike the modern household, ancient households included not only a married couple and children but also other dependents, such as slaves, with the head of the household in a position of authority to which wife, children, and slaves were to submit. The New Testament includes several "household codes" (esp. Eph. 5:21–6:9; Col. 3:18–4:1), lists that address the various members of the household as to their duties, usually progressing from the "lesser" (i.e., the one under authority) to the "greater" (i.e., the one in a position of authority). The underlying assumption of such codes is that order in the household will promote order on a larger societal scale as well. Believers' conformance to the ethical standards of a code would render Christianity respectable in the surrounding culture (1 Tim. 3:7; 6:1; Titus 2:5, 8, 10; 3:8; 1 Pet. 2:12) and aid in the church's evangelistic mission (1 Thess. 4:12).[19] In keeping with the Pauline pattern, we will comment first on the subordinate group, that is, children, and then proceed to discuss parents, both fathers and mothers.

Children in Paul's Teaching

As mentioned, in the Old Testament honoring one's parents is mandated, while disobedience toward one's parents is put on the same level as treason and idol worship (see, e.g., Ex. 21:15, 17; Lev. 19:3; 20:9; Deut. 21:18–21; 27:16). First-century Jews, too, prized obedience in children. It was recognized, however, that such obedience could not be assumed to arise naturally but must be inculcated from childhood. Ultimately, the standing and honor of the entire family was at stake. What is more, the hand of divine blessing could be withdrawn if God's commandment to honor one's parents and his injunction for parents to raise their children in the nurture and admonition of the Lord were disregarded. Hence, the man of God must see to it "that his children obey him with proper respect" (1 Tim. 3:4 NIV; see Titus 1:6). In the New

Testament, disobedience toward parents is viewed as a phenomenon characteristic of the end times (Mark 13:12; 2 Tim. 3:1–2; see 1 Tim. 1:9) that would draw divine judgment (Rom. 1:30, 32).

The apostle Paul considered children's obedience to be vital. The major Pauline injunction pertaining to children is found as part of the "household code" in Ephesians 6:1–3: "Children, obey your parents in the Lord, for this is right. 'Honor your father and mother' (this is the first commandment with a promise), 'that it may go well with you and that you may live long in the land.'" While the commandment to honor one's parents is cited five other times in the New Testament (Matt. 15:4; 19:19; Mark 7:10; 10:19; Luke 18:20), the attached promise is cited only in Ephesians. Paul's words in Colossians 3:20–21 are similar: "Children, obey your parents in everything, for this pleases the Lord. Fathers, do not provoke your children, lest they become discouraged."

In the more extensive passage in Ephesians, Paul indicates that children's submission to their parents is a result of Spirit-filling (Eph. 6:1; see Eph. 5:18), which suggests that only regenerate children can consistently live out this pattern of relationship in the power of the Holy Spirit.[20] Why ought children to obey their parents? By the phrase "this is right" in Ephesians 6:1, Paul roots children's obligation to obey their parents in the Old Testament Decalogue (Ex. 20:12 lxx; see Deut. 5:16). Interestingly, the command to honor one's parents follows immediately after the first four commandments (which have to do with God's holiness) as the first commandment that relates to right relationships between human beings on a horizontal level.

In the Ephesians passage, Paul treats children as responsible members of the congregation whose obedience to their parents "is all of a piece with their submission to Christ."[21] The phrase "in the Lord" in Ephesians 6:1 is equivalent to "as to the Lord" or "as to Christ" (see Eph. 5:22; 6:5) and indicates that children's obedience is part of their Christian discipleship. Obedience means honor, respect, and, properly understood, "fear" of one's parents

(Lev. 19:3; see Lev. 19:14). In the context of the present passage, children's obedience to their parents epitomizes a submission that arises from a godly fear of Christ himself (Eph. 5:21).

The promise that it will go well with children who honor their parents referred in the original context (Ex. 20:12) to long life in the (promised) land of Israel. Paul universalizes the promise and thus indicates its continued relevance and applicability. No longer is the promise limited geographically; obedient children are promised a long life on earth wherever they may live. Ephesians 6:1–3 appears to be addressed primarily to children who are in the process of learning and growing up or at least old enough that they could be "provoked to anger" (see Eph. 6:4).[22] However, while children's responsibilities toward their parents change once they establish their own families, they do not therefore cease. In a later letter, Paul notes that children's responsibility to honor their parents also entails caring for them in their old age (1 Tim. 5:8), which is viewed as proper repayment for having been reared by them (1 Tim. 5:4).

It is critical that parents teach children the importance of obedience. Parents who neglect to hold their children accountable for rendering obedience fail them in that they do not help them along the path of Christian discipleship, of which obedience is a central component. Hence the primary importance of obedience is not for parents to receive their children's obedience, but for parents to help children to learn to exercise obedience ultimately *in their relationship with God*. The fact that proper obedience is possible, for children as well as for adults, ultimately only as a result of a faith commitment to Jesus Christ and in the power of the Holy Spirit, suggests that introducing the child to a personal relationship with God in Christ ought to be a burning fire in the heart of every Christian parent. Nevertheless, obedience should be demanded and disobedience punished, even in non-Christian (as of yet) children.

Fathers and the Importance of Fatherhood in Paul's Teaching

In Ephesians 6:4, Paul writes, "Fathers, do not provoke your children to anger, but bring them up in the discipline and instruction of the Lord." The Colossian parallel reads, "Fathers, do not provoke your children, lest they become discouraged" (Col. 3:21). While children ought to obey both parents (Eph. 6:1; Col. 3:20), fathers bear special responsibility for disciplining their children and are specifically singled out by Paul in the present passage. Although mothers may actually spend more time with them, the father is given the primary responsibility for disciplining his children. The apostle's exhortation to fathers not to exasperate (Eph. 6:4 NIV) their children echoes his earlier concern about anger in Ephesians 4:26–27, 31, while the positive injunction to bring up children in the training and admonition of the Lord recalls the earlier emphasis on learning Christian teaching in Ephesians 4:20–21.[23]

Fathers must not provoke their children to anger (Eph. 6:4; also see Eph. 4:26–27, 31). If anger is prolonged, Satan will seek to exploit the familial discord to further his own ends. Fathers are therefore to avoid any attitudes, words, or actions that have the effect of provoking anger in their children, including "excessively severe discipline, unreasonably harsh demands, abuse of authority, arbitrariness, unfairness, constant nagging and condemnation, subjecting a child to humiliation, and all forms of gross insensitivity to a child's needs and sensibilities."[24] Children are persons with dignity in their own right. They are not slaves owned by their parents but are entrusted to them by God as a sacred stewardship. In the Colossians passage, Paul notes that as a result of improper treatment, children may become discouraged (Col. 3:21). Indeed, few things are more heartbreaking than a child who has "lost heart" because of poor parenting.

Positively, fathers are to bring up their children "in the discipline and instruction of the Lord." The term "bring up" or "nourish," used in Ephesians 5:29 for Christ's nurture of his church, conveys the sense of rearing children to maturity, which includes, but is not limited to, providing for their physical and psychological needs. "Discipline" and "instruction" are closely related but probably not synonymous. In its New Testament usage, the term translated "discipline" may refer to education or training in general (Acts 7:22; 22:3; 2 Tim. 3:16; Titus 2:1) or specifically to chastisement for wrongdoing (1 Cor. 11:32; 2 Cor. 6:9; Heb. 12:5, 7, 8, 11). In Ephesians 6:4, the reference is in all likelihood to training in general, while encompassing discipline for wrongdoing as well. The phrase "of the Lord" (Eph. 6:4) implies that fathers themselves must be Christian disciples, so that they can raise their children and administer discipline in a way that is truly and thoroughly Christian.

Looking at other relevant New Testament references, we observe that fathers' primary role is to provide for their children and to ensure proper nurture and discipline. This involves formal as well as informal education and entails the exercise of various forms of discipline, including physical discipline (Prov. 13:24; 22:15; 23:13–14; Heb. 12:6; Rev. 3:19). As in the Greco-Roman world where the father's authority held unrivaled sway in his household, in both Jewish culture and biblical teaching the father ought to command great respect. As mentioned, however, fathers are not to use their position of authority to exasperate their children, but to treat them with gentleness (1 Cor. 4:15, 21; 1 Thess. 2:11; Col. 3:21; Eph. 6:4).

Mothers and the Importance of Motherhood in Paul's Teaching

The apostle Paul taught that one of the primary roles of women is that of "childbearing," that is, not only the act of giving birth but their domestic role related to the upbringing of children and managing of the home (1 Tim. 2:15; see 5:14). Thus, motherhood is not disparaged in biblical teaching; contrary to modern society, it is held up as the woman's highest calling and privilege. In fact, in his first letter to Timothy, the apostle intimates that, for women, straying from the home is yielding to the Devil's temptation in a similar way to Eve overstepping her bounds at the original fall (1 Tim. 2:14–15).[25]

First Timothy 2:15 speaks a powerful message to our culture "where many are seeking to 'liberate' women from all encumbrances of family responsibilities in order to unleash them on a quest for self-fulfillment apart from such functions."[26] To the contrary, "it is precisely by participating in her role pertaining to the family that women fulfill their central calling."[27] Women's obedience will result not only in greater blessing and fulfillment for themselves but also for their husbands and families, and it will bring honor to the God who created us male and female.

The Importance of Older Women's Mentoring Younger Women

In his letter to Titus, Paul delineates the duties of both older and younger Christian women.

Older women must be treated with respect (1 Tim. 5:1–2), and they have the important obligation to mentor younger women with regard to their family responsibilities (Titus 2:3–5). Older women are to exemplify the following four characteristics: (1) to be reverent in the way they live; (2) not to be slanderers; (3) not to be addicted (literally, "bound" or "enslaved") to much wine;[28] and (4) to be "teachers of the good." Older women who avoided slander and wine were sure to stand out in their immoral Cretan surroundings (the destination of Paul's epistle to Titus). The restricted movement often brought about by advanced age makes older people (then as today) particularly susceptible to fill their days with pastimes such as drinking or gossiping; this calls for godliness and self-control.

Older women are to cultivate virtue, not as an end in itself but for the purpose of training young women (see 1 Tim. 5:2). Nevertheless, it is impossible to train others in qualities oneself does not possess. There is a great need in the contemporary church for older women who are godly and who obey the biblical command to train young women in the faith. Many younger women long for more mature women to take them under their wings and to teach them how to live the Christian life, especially since many of them lack such godly models in their own families or live at a great distance from home. Notably, such training—usually involving private rather than public instruction—is to focus squarely on the domestic sphere.

Paul groups instructions for younger women in three pairs plus one final general injunction, starting and ending with their relationship to their husbands (Titus 2:4–5). First, they are to be *certain kinds of wives and mothers*: lovers of their husbands and lovers of their children (Titus 2:4). Second, they are to be *cultivating Christian character*: self-controlled and pure (Titus 2:5; see 1 Tim. 5:22; 2 Cor. 11:2; Phil. 4:8; 1 Pet. 3:2; 1 John 3:3). Third, they are to be engaged in activities with the *right kind of attitude*: workers at home (Titus 2:5; see 1 Tim. 5:14) and kind (literally "good"; see 1 Thess. 5:15; Eph. 4:32). Finally, they are to be *subject to their own husbands* (see Eph. 5:24; Col. 3:18; 1 Pet. 3:1, 5).

PRACTICAL IMPLICATIONS

Children, like all people, are spiritual individuals who are uniquely created by God and yet are fallen sinners. Thus the task of parenting is not merely that of behavioral conditioning but spiritual nurture and training. The use of one particular methodology in the exercise of external discipline or parental drills has some value but is limited in its usefulness. An engagement of the root cause of all unrighteous human behavior, sin, should be the goal (see Rom. 3:23; 6:23). In reality, only those children and young people who experience personal regeneration through faith in Christ and receive the indwelling Holy Spirit can truly and permanently live a life pleasing to God and benefit as their parents guide them toward greater wisdom. This, however, does not do away with the need for parental discipline and training prior to a child's conversion. It does mean, though, that parental efforts can only go so far unless aided by the internal, supernatural enablement in the response of the child. Thus the child's conversion is truly an important aspect of parental guidance.

For this reason also parents ought not to be surprised or shocked when their children disobey. *Of course* children will disobey—they are sinners! Parents rather should be expecting their children to sin, even after they have come to faith in Christ. Such an expectation is realistic and enables the parent to deal with each infraction calmly and deliberately, administering discipline with fairness, justice, and consistency (see Eph. 6:4; Col. 3:21). Whether or not they are believers, children need their parents to set and enforce standards for right and wrong behavior. This is how children learn to assume responsibility for their actions and come to realize that there are consequences for obedience as well as for disobedience. Hence the parents' role is both positive and negative, similar to the effect of Scripture in a person's life—they must teach and train their children in righteousness, but they must also discipline and correct (2 Tim. 3:16–17).

The role of the parent in the life of a converted child is not that of a substitute for the Holy Spirit (though prior to a child's conversion, the parent may have a more direct role in convicting the child of sin). Nor can parents ultimately make moral choices *for* their children. Parents ought to consider themselves entrusted with the (temporary) responsibility and stewardship of nurturing and cultivating a child's heart and mind in light of the Scriptures and on behalf of God (Ps. 127:3; 128:3–4). This also entails respect for the child's individuality and unique creation in the eyes of God (Ps. 139:13–14). Every child is different and unique, and parental techniques that may work well with one child may not work as well with another.

In all these cases, therefore, there is no substitute for the Holy Spirit's leading in each individual situation. Parents should prayerfully search the Scriptures and team up with other families that live nearby and with other Christian parents in their church. Talking to one another in order to arrive at a joint parenting philosophy is essential for a married couple so that they are unified in their approach and are pulling together rather than moving in different directions. In addition, parents should make the necessary adjustments in their approach to parenting along the way.

To be sure, no human parent is adequate to this task apart from God's help, nor are children able to pursue these characteristics apart from divine enablement. Parents occasionally may need to ask forgiveness from their children, which may help the children to understand that their parents are sinners, too. Parents should model a prayerful attitude of dependence on God in all things so that children come to realize that even their parents and other adults have limitations and need God's help. Finally, joint worship, both as part of a local congregation and as a family at home, is a vital part of knitting a family together as brothers and sisters in Christ.

4

REPRODUCTION
AND PARENTING

At the beginning, the Creator charged the man and the woman to "be fruitful and multiply and fill the earth and subdue it" (Gen. 1:28). However, in this fallen world, things are rarely this simple. In fact, issues related to human reproduction today are vast, including childlessness and related medical issues, abortion, contraception, artificial reproductive technologies, and adoption. For those with children, parenting in today's world is likewise fraught with challenges and opportunities. In this chapter, we will take a closer look at many of these pressing issues with which we are confronted in this critical area of our lives.

REPRODUCTION
Childlessness and Related Medical Issues
There is perhaps no one who can better appreciate the value of children today than a woman who is unable to conceive and who desperately wants to have children of her own. Not that childless couples or single persons are not in the will of God or cannot make significant contributions to the kingdom; physical fruitfulness is but a part of God's overall desire for humans to be fruitful; he desires spiritual fruitfulness as well (see John 15:8, 16). Nevertheless, the bearing and raising of children remains a vital part of the divine design for men and women today. God's overarching plan for humanity to "be fruitful and multiply" has

numerous contemporary implications covering a wide range of issues, such as abortion, contraception, infertility, and adoption.

Abortion

Abortion is not a practice condoned by Scripture, as evidenced by its general teaching regarding the value of human life and on the basis of specific passages. Both Testaments teach that children are a blessing from God (Ps. 127:3–5; Mark 10:13–16) and regard the killing of children with particular horror (e.g., Ex. 1:16–17, 22; Lev. 18:21; Jer. 7:31–32; Ezek. 16:20–21; Mic. 6:7; Matt. 2:16–18; Acts 7:19). God is shown to be active in the creation of human beings from the time of conception (Old Testament examples include births to Sarah [Gen. 17:15–22; 21:1–7], Leah, Rachel [Gen. 30:1–24], Ruth [Ruth 4:13–17], and Hannah [1 Sam. 1:19–20]; in the New Testament, see esp. Elizabeth in Luke 1:24–25, 39–44), so that human procreation in fact represents "a co-creative process involving man, woman and God."[1] The psalmist provides a particularly moving tribute to God's involvement in creating a human being even in the mother's womb:

> For you formed my inward parts;
>> you knitted me together in my mother's womb.
> I praise you, for I am fearfully and wonderfully made.
> Wonderful are your works;
>> my soul knows it very well.
> My frame was not hidden from you,
> when I was being made in secret,
>> intricately woven in the depths of the earth.
> Your eyes saw my unformed substance;
> in your book were written, every one of them,
>> the days that were formed for me,
>> when as yet there was none of them. (Ps. 139:13–16)

Another biblical passage makes clear that God forms the fetus in the womb and that in fact he has personal knowledge of the unborn child: "Before I *formed you* in the womb I *knew you*, and before you were born I consecrated you; I appointed you a prophet to the nations" (Jer. 1:5; see also Job 10:9–12; 31:15; Ps. 119:73; Eccles. 11:5). While the Old Testament does not provide any theoretical discussion as to whether a fetus is a "person," it does "depict the fetus as the work of God and the object of his knowledge, love, and care, and hence its destruction must be considered contrary to the will of God."[2]

The Old Testament's "profound respect for life in the prenatal stage" is also revealed by the Mosaic stipulation that the one who harms an unborn child in his or her mother's womb must be punished "life for life, eye for eye, tooth for tooth, hand for hand, foot for foot, burn for burn, wound for wound, stripe for stripe" (Ex. 21:22–25).[3] All of these passages clearly imply that Scripture views human life as beginning at conception and that there is no such thing as a "human right" to take the life of an unborn child. This is in keeping with the biblical affirmation that God is a God of life and that everything he created (especially human beings) is precious and worth preserving (e.g., Psalm 8). In this regard, Scripture differs markedly from ancient pagan cultures.

While abortion was often attempted in the ancient world, more common was the exposure of a newborn child after birth. One of the main reasons why abortion was not as common is that mothers would likely have died as a result. Also, boys were valued more highly than girls, so people waited until after the birth to see whether the child was a boy or a girl. If it was the latter, the choice was often to expose the poor infant. Such an exposed child was left to die on a trash heap or in some isolated location. In the Greco-Roman world, exposure was not considered infanticide but refusal to admit to society, which did not carry negative moral implications.

The early Christians, following the lead of the Jews, likewise condemned abortion and exposure. In the *Didache*, an ancient manual of church instruction, we read, "'You shall not commit murder . . . ': you shall not procure abortion, nor commit infanticide" (*Did.* 2:2). The *Letter of Barnabas* states similarly, "Thou shalt not procure abortion, thou shalt not commit infanticide" (*Ep. Barn.* 19:5). Justin writes, "But as for us, we have been taught that to expose newly-born children is the part of wicked men . . . , first, because we see that almost all so exposed . . . are brought up to prostitution" (*1 Apol.* 1.27). The *Letter to Diognetus* describes Christians as follows: "They marry as all men, they bear children, but they do not expose their offspring" (*Ep. Diogn.* 5:6).[4]

It is not our purpose here to address the contemporary debate regarding abortion directly. As the above-cited biblical and extra-biblical passages make clear, however, the ancient world witnessed a marked difference between the pagan world and Judeo-Christian teaching on the subject. While certain aspects of complexity have been introduced into the modern discussion, many of the pertinent issues were already addressed in the first centuries of the Christian era (and even prior to this period). As the preceding survey has shown, the view that life begins at conception has been the traditional Judeo-Christian view, and this view alone seems to do justice to the teaching of Scripture and the life and practice of the early church. For this reason abortion must be considered the unauthorized taking of a preborn human life, which is contrary to God's will.

Contraception (by Mark Liederbach)

Scripture does not speak directly to the question of whether it is biblically appropriate to use contraceptive measures. There is no explicit biblical passage that mentions the term *contraception*, nor are there any plain texts that specifically address the issue of whether it might be appropriate to use contraceptive measures. This said, however, one should not assume that Scripture is completely silent on the matter.

The Question of the Legitimacy of Contraception in General

As noted above, Genesis 1:28 identifies procreation as a primary end of the marital union, while Psalm 127 describes children as a blessing from God. Thus, when considering the question of whether to use contraception, one must start from the perspective that having children is the expected norm for marriages and should be understood as a good gift from a loving heavenly Father.

Having recognized the important connection between sexual expression and childbearing, however, does it follow that every act of sexual intercourse must "be open" to procreation? Those who answer this question in the affirmative will often cite the Genesis 38:6–10 account of Onan and Tamar in support of their position. In this passage, God takes the life of Er, the oldest son of Judah, because he was "evil in the sight of the Lord" (NASB) leaving his wife Tamar a widow. The Hebrew custom known as levirate marriage (Deut. 25:5–10) stipulated that when a married man died without leaving offspring, his widow should marry the dead man's next closest male relative. The first child from that subsequent marriage would take on the name of the first husband and become his heir so that the name of the deceased man "will not be blotted out from Israel" (Deut. 25:6 NIV). In the present instance, however, Onan, as Er's next oldest brother, failed to take on the responsibility of providing Tamar with a child. According to Genesis 38:9, while Onan did indeed have sexual intercourse with Tamar, instead of providing an heir for her first husband, Scripture indicates that he "wasted his seed on the ground" (NASB). As a result, his action was "displeasing in the sight of the Lord," and God took his life as well (Gen. 38:10 NASB).

Roman Catholics typically cite this passage to suggest that what particularly displeased the Lord was the interruption of the sexual process for the purpose of preventing procreation. Every act of sexual intercourse, it is argued, ought to be open to procreation. Thus, the interruption by Onan, as well as any form of interruption or use of artificial means to prevent conception during sexual intercourse, is morally reprehensible. In their view, all means of contraception that interrupt the natural process of procreation are contrary to God's will.[5]

Upon closer scrutiny, however, it appears that the Lord's displeasure in Genesis 38:10 ought not to be equated with the prevention of pregnancy *per se* but with the particularly exploitive, abusive, and wasteful way in which Onan carried out his sexual relations with Tamar. Deuteronomy 25:5–10 indicates that if the brother refuses to complete his "duty" to provide an offspring, the penalty is not death but shaming (Deut. 25:9–10). It would appear, then, that the severity of the punishment indicates that reasons besides the refusal to provide an offspring for his deceased brother prompted God to take Onan's life.

How, then, ought one to reason biblically with regard to contraception? As mentioned, Scripture indicates that, in addition to procreation, God created marriage to meet other ends as well, including companionship (Gen. 2:18, 20) and sexual pleasure (Prov. 5:15–23; Song of Solomon). Therefore, while it seems clear that over the course of their marriage a couple ought to seek to have children (perhaps even many, see Ps. 127:5), it does not follow that *in every particular sexual encounter* the couple must refrain from the use of contraception. The sexual encounter in marriage retains a high value for the purposes of union, pleasure, fidelity, and so on, even in the event that a couple uses contraception as a part of their family planning. Indeed, "the focus on 'each and every act' of sexual intercourse within a faithful marriage that is open to the gift of children goes beyond the biblical demand."[6]

Morally Permissible and Impermissible Forms of Contraception

Which forms of birth control are morally acceptable? In answering this question it is important to remember that the "profound respect for life in the prenatal stage" found in the Judeo-Christian ethic must also influence one's perspective on which forms of birth control are biblically permissible. In short, then, the answer is *only those that are contraceptive in nature, that is, those that exclusively prohibit conception.* Resting on this foundational principle, one can then fairly easily evaluate which forms of family planning are appropriate and which are not.

Acceptable forms include natural methods such as *abstinence* (the only biblically legitimate option for those who are not married) and the *rhythm or calendar method* (in its various forms such as relying on body temperature cycles or timing of ovulation and fertility periods). In addition, artificial methods that exclusively seek to prevent conception are also morally acceptable. These include *barrier methods* such as a diaphragm, a cervical cap, and condoms and spermicides such as foams, creams, sponges, or vaginal suppositories.

Unacceptable forms of family planning include all forms of induced abortion. Thus, the intrauterine device, or IUD, is an unacceptable method because its primary function is to create an unstable environment for the fertilized egg to implant in the uterine wall. It depletes the endometrial lining, making it incapable of supporting the life of the child. RU-486, or the so-called abortion or morning-after pill, is likewise morally unacceptable since its primary function is to prevent the implantation of a new fetus in the uterine wall. The drug works to directly prohibit the establishment and continuation of the pregnancy by blocking the body's natural secretion of progesterone, the vital hormone that prepares the uterus to receive a fertilized egg and to help maintain the pregnancy once it occurs.

Methods Requiring Special Mention and Extra Care

Sterilization as a means of contraception involves a surgical procedure designed to permanently terminate a person's fertility. For the male, a vasectomy blocks the *vas deferens* (ejaculatory duct) and thus prevents the sperm from leaving the body during ejaculation. For the female, tubal occlusion is the procedure that effectively blocks a woman's fallopian tubes in order to prevent sperm from coming into contact with the woman's egg, thereby preventing fertilization.

Several important considerations with sterilization may caution us against its use. First, as an elective procedure it involves the intentional and permanent setting aside or inactivation of a bodily function. Second, the permanence of the procedure makes it a different case from the use of a condom or other temporary measures. Finally, we might ask whether it is ever right to remove a part of one's body (see Lev. 21:20; Deut. 23:1; 1 Cor. 6:19) simply for convenience's sake, and whether this is the proper way to treat the body as the "temple of the Holy Spirit" (1 Cor. 6:19).

The question, then, becomes whether sterilization is a legitimate means of ensuring that no additional children are conceived. In light of our conclusion that it is fallacious to interpret the command to "be fruitful and multiply" to mean that every act of marital sexual intercourse must be open to procreation, it would seem appropriate that a given couple could determine that they have reached the point where they believe God would not have them conceive any more children. It is imperative, however, that a couple who would use a given method honestly search their hearts and motives during the process of making such a decision and be certain that pragmatic considerations and personal desires do not override scriptural principles or unduly shape what they perceive to be the leading of the Holy Spirit.

Another birth control method requiring special mention and extra care is that popularly known as "the pill." Because of its wide acceptance in the culture, some Christians may be surprised to learn that the moral acceptability of the pill (and the many various applications of the same basic chemical products, such as patches, implants, rings, and injections) is under question by Christian ethicists. Yet, while the convenience and effectiveness of this form of birth control have certainly commended it to many, serious moral questions must be addressed before a decision is made as to whether the pill qualifies as an acceptable form of contraception.

There are two basic categories of hormonally based chemical contraceptives: combined and progestin-only contraceptives.

According to the *Physician's Desk Reference*, both combined contraceptives and progestin-only contraceptives work by employing the same three basic mechanisms of action. The first of these is to prevent ovulation (a contraceptive mechanism). The second is to alter the cervical mucus buildup, which increases the difficulty of the sperm entering the uterus and thereby fertilizing the egg (a contraceptive mechanism). The third mechanism—in all forms of both combined contraceptives and progestin-only contraceptives—whether intended or not, is to inhibit the *endometrium* (uterine lining), thereby making it incapable of supporting the life of the newly conceived child should fertilization take place. This third mechanism, then, is not a contraceptive measure but an *abortifacient*; that is, the mechanism works as a fail-safe means to control birth if the other two mechanisms do not prevent conception.

To summarize, with regard to both the combined contraceptives and progestin-only contraceptives, the main moral problem occurs when the first and second mechanisms of action fail (prevention of ovulation and of fertilization due to mucus buildup), and fertilization of an egg takes place. At this point these methods cease to be contraceptive in nature and function as abortifacients. While the chances of the first two methods failing are admittedly low, given the fact that so many women are using these forms of birth control, there is no question that for some the pill or its equivalents are functioning at least at times to terminate the life of a conceived child. Indeed, if the "profound respect for life in the prenatal stages" of a child's development discussed earlier holds the moral authority it ought to, then perhaps it is right to reevaluate whether a low chance of aborting one's child is worth the risk at all.

Artificial Reproductive Technologies (ART) (by Mark Liederbach)
The Challenge of Infertility
In light of the clear scriptural mandate for couples to "be fruitful and multiply" (Gen. 1:28), one of the more difficult trials a

married couple can face is the inability to have children.[7] The Old Testament records the agonizing emotions and experiences of both Sarah (Genesis 15–17) and Hannah (1 Sam. 1:1–11) as they struggled with their experiences of infertility. The New Testament, likewise, indicates that Elizabeth remained childless well into her old age (Luke 1:7). In each of these cases, God was gracious and allowed the women to conceive and bear children who would in due course play major roles in his redemptive plan. Arguably, however, God does not always act through miraculous means to overcome a couple's infertility.

In recent years, advances in modern reproductive technology have paved the way for otherwise infertile couples to give birth to children of their own. In light of these advances, how should Christians respond? Is it appropriate to take advantage of these new technologies? Some argue that prayer and faith alone are the proper response of Christians in the face of infertility.[8] Most Christians, however, relying on the fact that God created human beings with the ability to reason and gave them dominion over the earth (Gen. 1:28–31), do not reject the use of medical intervention as long as the type of intervention does not violate other clear principles of Scripture (i.e., the sanctity of human life). In what follows we will first provide a brief description of each of the major artificial reproductive technologies and then discuss the various ethical issues involved by using four important guiding principles.

Description of Methods

Intrauterine insemination (IUI), which is also known as *artificial insemination* (AI), is usually the first option chosen by infertile couples when the problem of infertility resides chiefly in the male. The usual problem is either low sperm count or, for whatever reason, defective sperm. Relatively simple in nature, this procedure involves the collection and accumulation of male sperm and then the injection of that sperm (usually with a needleless syringe) into the female uterus during the most fertile part of a woman's cycle. The hope, then, is that the reproductive process will proceed from that point along "natural" lines. This procedure can take place with either the husband's sperm (AIH: artificial insemination husband) or a donor's sperm (AID: artificial insemination donor). Ethically speaking, there are far fewer problems with AIH than AID.

Gamete intrafallopian transfer (GIFT) is the procedure by which female eggs are harvested through the use of super-ovulatory hormonal drugs stimulating the maturation and release of several eggs. These eggs are then harvested by means of a minor surgical procedure utilizing ultrasound guidance in the vagina. The male semen that is also collected is treated to make it less viscous, facilitating the conception process. These gametes are then placed together in a single catheter, separated only by a tiny air bubble, and placed together in the woman's fallopian tubes. The procedure facilitates the reproductive process by assuring contact between egg and sperm and thus raising the probability that conception will occur and pregnancy begin.

In vitro fertilization (IVF) is very similar to GIFT in technical procedure but has one major distinction. While in the GIFT procedure fertilization and conception take place within a woman's body, in the case of IVF fertilization takes place in an artificial environment (*in vitro* literally means "in glass," referring to the test tube or petri dish where conception occurs). As with GIFT, the woman receives hormonal treatments in order to stimulate the release of multiple eggs, which are then harvested for use in the procedure. Male sperm is also collected, and these gametes (eggs and sperm) are then placed in the same petri dish in hopes that multiple conceptions will occur. The reproductive technician will then screen the newly formed embryos and, via *embryo transfer* (ET), will attempt to implant as many as four of the embryos into the woman's uterus in hopes that she will become pregnant with at least one. The remaining embryos will then be either destroyed or frozen for use in future birthing attempts. Studies indicate that roughly 25 percent of the frozen embryos will not survive the freezing and thawing process prior to the next attempt.[9]

Surrogacy or *surrogate motherhood* refers to the procedure in which the gestation and birth of a baby occur in a woman who either is not the child's biological mother or is willing to donate her egg and carry a child but relinquishes parenting rights to those contracting with her to carry the child. Thus "genetic surrogacy" results from an IUI procedure where the husband of a given couple donates his sperm in order for the surrogate to conceive, carry the child through gestation, and then give birth. While genetically related to the surrogate mother, this baby "belongs" to the couple that contracted with her to carry and birth the child. Gestational surrogacy differs from genetic surrogacy in that the conception of the child takes place via GIFT or IVF and the embryo is then placed by way of ET into the surrogate mother. The role of the surrogate in this case is to carry and give birth to the child, not to conceive or donate her egg. In both forms of surrogacy, the surrogate mother, in exchange for a fee, typically contracts to release all rights to parent the child once it is born.

Principles of Evaluation

As in the case of contraception, it is important to recognize that simply because a technology is available does not necessarily mean that it is ethically permissible to employ it. Rather, it is imperative to explore the available options with regard to how they align with biblical principles that ought to guide the decision-making process. In the matter of reproductive technologies, four principles are particularly germane.

First, as in the case of contraception, *respect for the sanctity of human life* directly relates to the issue of reproductive technologies, for the following reasons. Some forms of reproductive technology, such as cloning, pose a direct threat to the life of the child due to the inexact nature and development of the technology. Other forms of reproductive technology may not directly threaten life, but the manner in which they are employed does. For example, it is common practice in certain methods of artificial insemination or in vitro fertilization to fertilize five or six ova at a time. Each of the resulting conceptions is a child waiting to be placed in a woman's uterus in order to grow toward birth. Unfortunately, it is also common practice for the doctors to select only one or two of these fertilized eggs for implantation, leaving the others to be destroyed.

Another way a reproductive technology threatens the sanctity of life is when the technique used (such as artificial insemination or the use of fertility drugs) results in a multichild pregnancy. In such cases, a woman may now be carrying four or five children in her womb. Because there is greater risk of miscarrying under these conditions, reproductive specialists will often recommend a procedure known as "selective reduction." While often described as a means to increase the chances that some of the babies may be born alive, the term "selective reduction" is in reality nothing more than a form of abortion in which one or more of the children are killed in order to increase the odds of the others' proceeding to live birth.

Thus, in such procedures (artificial insemination, in vitro fertilization) a couple must be willing to have all the conceptions implanted and carried to full term in order for this technology to meet the biblical standards with regard to the sanctity of life (with the possible exception of instances where the life of the mother is at stake). Likewise, those using fertility drugs must recognize ahead of time that a multiple-child birth is a possibility and that "selective reduction" is not a biblically legitimate option.

A second biblical principle that must be considered is that of *respect for all human beings as image bearers*. Because all humans bear the image of God (Gen. 1:27), it is wrong to use or treat another as a means to an end only or to purposely put them in harm's way when they have not incurred guilt and when there is no other reason than convenience for such a choice. Once again, in the case of some forms of reproductive technologies, it is common practice to fertilize several eggs and then freeze these children for an indefinite amount of time to be used or discarded if the parents opt to forgo having any more children. Such practices are inherently disrespectful and use these children merely as a means to the parents' chosen goals and must therefore be discarded as inappropriate avenues for Christians to pursue.

A third guiding principle for determining the moral value of a given reproductive technology is *respect for the fidelity of the marital bond*. Genesis 2:24 states that a man is to "leave his father and his mother and hold fast to his wife, and they shall become one flesh." It is within the context of this one-flesh relationship of husband and wife that God gave the command to be fruitful and multiply. Likewise, Scripture elsewhere not only condemns adulterous relationships (Ex. 20:14; Deut. 5:18; Rom. 13:9) but also affirms the exclusive nature of the marital bond (Matt. 19:5; 1 Cor. 6–7; Eph. 5:28–31). This biblical emphasis on the unity and exclusivity of the marital bond has direct implications on the use of reproductive technologies, particularly those methods that utilize the genetic material (donor egg, donor sperm, donor DNA) from someone other than the husband or wife. Because the use of donor egg or sperm introduces into the marriage (specifically the sexually related area) sexually related genetic material of a third person, there is considerable doubt with regard to the morality of such a practice.

While one would be hard-pressed to place this in the exact category of what society has historically understood to be adultery, one could easily argue that using a donor egg or sperm is tantamount to adultery or at the very least an inappropriate intrusion upon the exclusive nature of marital fidelity and sexuality. As Scott Rae rightly points out, "the weight of biblical teaching suggests that third-party contributors are not the norm for procreation. Scripture looks skeptically on any reproductive intervention that goes outside the married couple for genetic material. That would mean that technologies such as donor insemination, egg donation, and surrogate motherhood are morally problematic."[10]

A fourth and final principle that ought to guide the evaluation of whether to use reproductive technologies relates not so much to the *form of technology* but to the *heart of the one wanting to use it*. While the desire to have and raise genetically related children is grounded in the created norms and cemented in God's imperative for us to "be fruitful and multiply," it is nonetheless important not to place one's hope or sense of worth too greatly on one's ability to have children. The final hope of the Christian does not lie in the ability to manipulate human reproductive systems or in the ability to have children at all. Whether through direct miraculous intervention (as in Hannah's case) or through the technological advancements made possible through the minds God has given us, children are a gift from God. Beyond this, Scripture indicates that our ultimate hope lies not in our ability to have children but rather in our Savior Jesus Christ.

In conclusion, then, while the use of reproductive technology may be *generally* permissible, one should not make the further assumption that *every form* of reproductive technology is therefore biblically and morally acceptable. Concerns for the respect for human life, human dignity, and fidelity to the marital bond need to govern one's evaluation of any particular form of reproductive technology. Indeed, once one considers the rather large ethical uncertainty and gray areas regarding many of these technologies (not to mention the financial costs), perhaps wisdom would suggest limiting one's efforts in this direction in favor of pursuing adoption.

Adoption

Both Testaments contain instances of adoption. In the Old Testament, Dan and Naphtali, and later Ephraim and Manasseh, were adopted by Jacob (Gen. 30:1–13; 48:5); Moses was adopted by

Pharaoh's daughter (Ex. 2:10); and Esther was adopted by Mordecai (Est. 2:7). In the New Testament, the most prominent example is Jesus's adoption by Joseph, who served as his earthly father, participating in his naming (Matt. 1:25), presenting him in the temple (Luke 2:22–24), protecting him from danger by taking him and his mother to Egypt (Matt. 2:13–15), and by teaching him a trade (Matt. 13:55; Mark 6:3). These biblical examples may serve as encouraging evidence for some married couples that the practice of adoption has honorable biblical precedent. Together with the metaphoric use of adoption in the New Testament, which will be discussed below, these passages show that adopted children are to be taken into the loving, intimate, and permanent context of a biblical marriage and family.[11]

In a spiritual sense, Paul teaches that believers are adopted into God's family as his sons and daughters (Rom. 8:15, 23; 9:4; Gal. 4:5; Eph. 1:5). The apostle develops this concept by appropriating Old Testament exodus typology and the messianic adoption formula in 2 Samuel 7:14 ("I will be a father to him and he will be a son to me" NASB; see Ps. 2:7) within the context of new-covenant theology. Just as Israel was redeemed and received her covenant privileges at the exodus (Ex. 4:22; Deut. 1:31; Hos. 11:1), so New Testament believers were redeemed from their slavery to sin in and through Christ, receiving their adoption as God's children (see 2 Cor. 6:18 citing 2 Sam. 7:14). Significantly, this will be fully realized only in the future at the final resurrection (Rom. 8:23).

While in Old Testament times certain ethnic constraints applied, believers are now "all sons of God through faith in Christ Jesus" (Gal. 3:26 NIV). If anyone belongs to Christ, he is Abraham's descendant and included in the promise (Gal. 3:28). This is a salvation-historical event of first-rate import: through adoption, believers are introduced into the filial relationship between Jesus the Son and God his Father, sharing together in the new family of God.[12] While the distinction between Jesus as the unique Son of God and believers as sons and daughters of God in Christ is not obliterated (e.g., John 20:17), believers nonetheless become in a real, spiritual sense brothers and sisters of Jesus as well as of one another (e.g., Heb. 2:11). Even fruitfulness is to some extent transformed from physical childbearing to the harmonious, productive operation of the various members of the body of Christ according to the spiritual gifts supplied by God the Spirit.[13]

PARENTING
Parenting Methods
The challenge of parenting raises a host of issues. One fundamental question is which method or childrearing philosophy parents will choose. Many popular resources on parenting focus on the proper administration of discipline. Advantages of this approach include a measure of predictability and consistency that comes with having a plan in place. Yet a rigid focus on method also has several downsides such as fostering a false sense of security and shifting the emphasis away from people to abstract principles.

In the end, a proper approach to parenting needs to leave adequate room for the *relational* component in parenting, taking into account the individuality of each child. It is, therefore, just one aspect of a Christian parenting philosophy that should be undergirded by *wisdom derived from meditation on Scripture, the filling of the Holy Spirit, advice from others* (including quality literature on Christian parenting), and *relational experience* with the child. Our supreme trust should be in God and in his Word, and we must humbly acknowledge that our understanding of Scripture is not to be equated with the teaching of Scripture itself.

In this relationship of parenting, there must be a balance of unconditional love, spiritual nurture, and discipline (Eph. 6:4) in a context of discipleship and Christian growth (2 Pet. 3:18). Likewise, biblical parenting requires that parents understand that both they and their children are fundamentally sinful. Children are not merely disobedient; they are disobedient *because* they are sinful. Hence, children ultimately need salvation, not merely parental discipline. Yet parents, too, are sinners, and so must guard against putting their own interests above those of their children. Self-interest parenting is driven by convenience, social status, and self-preservation that fall well short of the biblical ideal of parenting.

Single Parenting

Single parenthood as a result of divorce entails several difficulties for the custodial and the noncustodial spouse and for the children involved. First, children may (and frequently do) end up emotionally torn between the parents as a result of the marital breakup and its aftermath. This will in all likelihood have a negative effect on the psychological development of children of divorce. Not infrequently do those children feel guilt, as if they were responsible for the failure of their parents' marriage. Second, in most cases such children grow up without a distinct and ongoing maternal and paternal presence. Thus not only does one person have to fill the role of both mother and father, but that person also needs to act as provider. Discipline, too, becomes the sole responsibility of the single parent.

Single parenting was not part of God's intended purpose in the beginning. For this reason biblical teaching on single parenting is elusive. Some affinity may exist between issues related to single parenting and scriptural passages pertaining to orphans and the fatherless on the one hand and to widows on the other, though there are obvious differences. Nevertheless, just as God is the God of the orphans and the widows, God's heart goes out in a special way to single parents who shoulder the load of being both father and mother to a child or several children. The Bible portrays God as the defender of the fatherless (Deut. 10:18; 27:19; Ps. 10:18; 82:3), as their sustainer and helper (Ps. 10:14; 146:9), and as their father (Ps. 68:5).[14] Because God himself serves as the protector and provider for the fatherless (as well as of widows and aliens), he commands his covenant people to do likewise. With sensitivity and empathy, individual believers and the church as a whole should seek to fill the void left by the absence of the other parent, provide financial support, or meet social and other needs.[15]

Physical Discipline

The point of departure for our discussion of physical discipline is the references in the book of Proverbs to the "rod" of correction, which is presented as serving three primary purposes: (1) as a means of disciplining a child based on parental love (Prov. 13:24); (2) as a way to remove folly and to impart wisdom (Prov. 22:15; 29:15); and (3) as a possible aid to the child's salvation (Prov. 23:13–14). The "rod" is mentioned in Proverbs also as a means of correcting or punishing fools (Prov. 10:13; 14:3; 22:8; 26:3).

Children need to learn the consequences of wrong behavior, and spanking can be a useful means to convey that lesson.[16] However, parents should take their child's unique personality and temperament into account and be aware that some children may respond better to alternative forms of positive or negative consequences and reinforcement (i.e., time-out, rewards, loss of privileges). Perhaps most importantly, what is needed is a comprehensive approach to parental discipline that is cognizant of the entire range of forms of discipline laid out in Scripture.[17]

The challenging task of raising and disciplining children requires great wisdom from Christian parents. In the end, parents are God's instruments in the lives of their children, and God's temporary agents in training their sons and daughters in the way they should go so that when they are old, they will not depart from it (Prov. 22:6). As Proverbs 3:11–12 states, "My son, do not despise the Lord's discipline, or be weary of his reproof, for the Lord reproves him whom he loves, as a father the son in whom he delights" (see Heb. 12:5–6).

While parenting cannot be reduced to a formula, Scripture does offer important instructions and guidelines for administering discipline. (1) To be effective, discipline must be *consistent*. (2) Discipline ought to be *age-appropriate* (Luke 2:51–52).

(3) Discipline must be *fair* and *just*. That is, *the punishment should fit the offense*. (4) Discipline should be *child-specific*. (5) Discipline should be administered in *love, not anger* (see Eph. 6:4; Col. 3:21). (6) Discipline should be *future-oriented* and *forward-looking*, aiming not so much at immediate compliance but at a child's long-term development into a mature and responsible Christian adult. (7) Discipline must be part of a *relationship* between parent and child that transcends any temporary form of discipline.

Cultivating Masculinity and Femininity

Another parenting issue that is of great contemporary relevance in light of the growing gender confusion in our culture is that of cultivating masculinity and femininity in our children. On a foundational level, it is important to realize that the biblical creation account indicates that sex and gender are not merely biological and sociological functions but that they define us as who we are as men and women in a much more thoroughgoing way.

In Genesis 1:27, we read that God created man in his own image as male and female. Yet while both the man and the woman were made in God's image, they were not made the same. As Genesis 2 makes clear, God first made the man and subsequently the woman as the man's "suitable helper" (Gen. 2:18, 20 NIV). Their union is presented not as unisex but as a partnership of two individuals who are distinct in their gender identity and thus complement one another.[18]

Nurturing boys' and girls' masculine and feminine identities is an important part of Christian parenting. As young people move toward marriage, men should take the initiative and women respond to their leadership. This is not merely a matter of traditional role division but an implication of the fact—attested by Scripture—that God put men in charge of both the home and the church and assigned to them the ultimate responsibility and authority for these institutions.

Marriage and the Family and Spiritual Warfare

Spiritual warfare has been a part of married life and childrearing from the beginning. The foundational biblical narrative in Genesis 3 recounts how the tempter, Satan, prevailed upon the first woman to violate God's commandment and how her husband followed her into sin. Ever since, marriage has resembled more a struggle for control and conscious and unconscious efforts at mutual manipulation than an Edenic paradise. The rest of the Old Testament chronicles a whole series of ways in which sin has affected marital and family relationships ever since the fall.

The message of the New Testament is no different. The most important treatment of spiritual warfare, Ephesians 6:10–20, is preceded by extended treatments of marriage (Eph. 5:21–33) and childrearing (Eph. 6:1–4). Unfortunately, these sections are regularly compartmentalized. In Paul's thinking, however, it is precisely in people's relationships with one another, be it at work or at home, among Christians or between believers and unbelievers, that spiritual warfare manifests itself, and conscious dealing with it becomes a necessity.

A Battle for the Mind

According to Scripture, the key element in spiritual warfare is human minds (2 Cor. 10:3–5; 11:3). For this reason believers ought to saturate their minds with scriptural teaching regarding their new position in Christ. Going no further than the book of Ephesians, we learn that we have been blessed with every spiritual blessing in Christ (Eph. 1:3). We were chosen in Christ to be holy and blameless (Eph. 1:4, 11). We were predestined to be adopted as his sons and daughters in Christ (Eph. 1:5, 11). We were redeemed and received forgiveness of sins through his blood (Eph. 1:7). We were given the Holy Spirit as a deposit guaranteeing their inheritance (Eph. 1:13–14). While we used to gratify the cravings of our sinful nature prior to our conversion to Christ (Eph. 2:3), we were raised up with Christ and seated with him in the heavenly realms

(Eph. 2:6). We have been saved by grace through faith (Eph. 2:8). On the basis of this understanding of our new position in Christ, we will be able to deal effectively with the various temptations and struggles with which we are confronted in our marriages and families.

The Devil's Toolbox: Sexual Temptation, Anger, and Insensitivity

The Devil's efforts to destroy marriages and to subvert family life did not stop at the fall but continue to this very day. The Devil has three particular tools in his toolbox. One is *sexual temptation*. Paul's remarks in 1 Corinthians 7:5 indicate that the sexual component of the marriage relationship is very much a regular target of Satan's attack and must be carefully guarded by the married couple.

A second area of weakness that Satan will target is *unresolved anger*. As Paul writes in Ephesians 4:26–27, "Do not let the sun go down while you are still angry, and do not give the devil a foothold" (NIV). While not limited to marriage, this pronouncement certainly includes the marriage relationship, cautioning believers not to allow broken relationships to render them vulnerable to the Devil. With regard to childrearing, fathers are enjoined not to provoke their children to anger lest they become discouraged (Eph. 6:4; Col. 3:21).

Third, Satan will seek to disrupt marriages by sowing the seeds of *marital conflict* through the *husband's insensitivity* to his wife. The apostle Paul tells husbands to love their wives and not to be harsh with them (Col. 3:19). Peter writes similarly, "Husbands, in the same way be considerate as you live with your wives, and treat them with respect as the weaker partner and as heirs with you of the gracious gift of life, so that nothing will hinder your prayers" (1 Pet. 3:7 NIV).

PRACTICAL IMPLICATIONS

How, then, are we to fight in this spiritual war in which we are engaged? Three important lessons emerge from the biblical teaching on spiritual warfare. First, an *awareness that there is a battle* is imperative. Anyone who, in the case of war, fails to realize that he is engaged in conflict will no doubt be an early casualty because of his failure to properly protect himself. It is the same in the realm of marriage.

Second, it is essential to *know one's spiritual enemy*. The enemy is not our spouse. Nor is it our children. It is Satan, the enemy of our souls, who employs a variety of strategies, methods, and schemes (see 2 Cor. 10:4; Eph. 6:11; 1 Pet. 5:8–9), including that of exploiting and inciting our sin nature and the sinful aspects of the godless world around us. Yet as with Paul, we will find that God's grace is more than sufficient for every challenge we face in the power of Christ.

Third, *spiritual battles must be fought by the use of proper weapons.* In the context of Christian marriages, as well as in parenting, it is imperative that we, in order to overcome a spiritual enemy—be it our own sinfulness or evil supernatural opposition—put on the "full armor of God" (Eph. 6:10–18 niv). What is more, we must not forget the larger context of the local church, which involves the principle of accountability and, if necessary, even church discipline.

SINGLENESS

Given the fact that 46 percent of the United States population over the age of fifteen was single at the beginning of the twenty-first century, the neglect and distortion of the state of singleness by the Western church is anything but justified.[1] Although most will eventually marry, statistics indicate that a growing number will never do so, and many who do will find themselves single once again because of divorce or the death of a spouse. For these reasons, and in light of the fact that many of the heroes of the Christian faith have been single (including Jesus)—not to mention the scriptural teaching that singleness can be a gracious gift of God (Matt. 19:11–12; 1 Cor. 7:7)—the contemporary church stands in urgent need of reappraising its stance on the issue of singleness.

SINGLENESS IN THE OLD TESTAMENT

In Old Testament times, singleness was rare among individuals old enough to marry, which was usually age twelve or thirteen for females and age fifteen or sixteen for males.[2] In fact, due largely to God's command to procreate (Gen. 1:28), people in Old Testament culture lacked the concept of anything akin to the contemporary notion of adolescence or the equivalent of an extended period of adult maturity without a spouse and children. Being single was viewed by the majority of people as living contrary to creation. Indeed, if someone was single in the Old Testament era, they generally fell into one of the following categories.

The first category of singles in the Old Testament era is that of *widows*. Like today, widowhood was not a desirable position in ancient times. Widows often faced financial struggles (see 2 Kings 4:1) and were certainly among the most helpless in ancient society (Deut. 10:18; Isa. 54:4).³ History reveals that because singleness was viewed as so unnatural, most widows sought to remarry as soon as possible, and many did remarry (e.g., Ruth 3–4). Yet, for widows who did not or could not remarry, the Lord made certain special provisions, such as the institution of levirate marriage (Deut. 25:5–6)⁴ and the concession that childless widows from priestly families could return to their father's household and partake of the priestly food (Lev. 22:13). In addition, God frequently reminded his people of their sacred duty to care for needy widows,⁵ and the Lord repeatedly described himself as a defender of widows.⁶ Nevertheless, widowhood was an unenviable position in Old Testament times that was largely looked upon as a reproach (Isa. 4:1). The concept of widowhood was even occasionally used by the Lord as a threatened punishment for Israel's spiritual disobedience (Isa. 47:8–9).

A second category of singles in the Old Testament era is that of *eunuchs*. Like those who found themselves widows, being a eunuch was not an enviable position in ancient times. Although eunuchs were part of many oriental royal courts, serving in positions such as keepers of virgins or concubines (Est. 2:3, 14–15), queens' attendants (Est. 4:5), confidants (Est. 1:12), overseers (Dan. 1:7), and even leaders in the military community (Jer. 52:25), for ancient Jews, being a eunuch would have been a detestable position, for it precluded one from the congregation of worshipers of the Lord (Deut. 23:1), as well as from participation in the priesthood (Lev. 21:20). Moreover, while several eunuchs in Old Testament times are presented in a "favorable" light, such as the three eunuchs that cast Jezebel out of her window to her death (2 Kings 9:32–33) and the sons mentioned by Isaiah who would serve in the palace of the king of Babylon (Isa. 39:7), eunuchs generally were looked upon with disdain. Becoming a eunuch was occasionally included in the threatened divine judgment for turning from the Lord (2 Kings 20:18; Isa. 39:7), and Isaiah notes that the Lord will remedy the unnatural state of eunuchs in the end times (Isa. 56:3–5).

A third category of singles in the Old Testament era was comprised of *those who could not marry* due to disease (e.g., leprosy) or severe economic difficulties.[7]

Fourth, there were those who did not marry because of some type of *divine call*. Perhaps the greatest example of an individual remaining single, at least for a time, because of a divine call is the prophet Jeremiah (though the command may have been due to the lack of suitable women "in this place"; Jer. 16:1–4). A divine call to or even a conscious choice of a lifetime of singleness, however, was rare in ancient times, as this is the only such example of an explicit divine call to singleness in the Old Testament.

A fifth category of singles in Old Testament times were the *divorced*.[8] Divorces were almost always initiated by the husband (Deut. 24:1–4; but see Judg. 19:1–2). Mosaic legislation sought to protect the divorced woman by requiring her husband to issue a certificate of divorce as legal proof of the dissolution of marriage. Similar to the death of a woman's spouse, divorce would put her in a very vulnerable economic position. Like a widow or orphan, the divorced woman would be left without male provision and protection. If unable to remarry, she would likely be economically destitute and in dire need of help from others.

The sixth and final category of singles in ancient Israel was *unmarried young men and women*. Fathers typically arranged for the marriage of their children to suitable partners (Genesis 24; Judges 14). They sought to protect their daughters from male predators to ensure that they would marry as virgins (see Ex. 22:16–17; Deut. 22:13–21) and provided their daughters with a dowry, which would be returned to the daughters if the marriage failed. As mentioned, in ancient Israel daughters tended to marry at the onset of puberty at about thirteen years of age, while sons would marry a couple of years later. For this reason there was hardly any interim between childhood and the married state that might meaningfully be termed "singleness."

SINGLENESS IN THE NEW TESTAMENT

As in Old Testament times, in the New Testament era singleness was not as clearly defined a concept as it is in the Western world today. If during the time of Christ a person was single, he or she more likely than not was in transition, whether that person was too young to marry, the death of a spouse had left the person widowed, or for some other reason. In New Testament times, singleness as a settled state and a conscious lifestyle choice was uncommon, and marriage was the norm.[9]

This said, John the Baptist, Jesus, and the apostle Paul were single, and despite the fact that there is comparatively little information on singleness in the New Testament, both Jesus and Paul refer to celibacy as being "eunuchs for the sake of the kingdom of heaven" (Matt. 19:12) or as a "gift from God" (1 Cor. 7:7), respectively. Jesus and Paul both indicate that such a call to celibacy allows unmarried persons to devote greater, more undistracted attention to religious service (Matt. 19:12; 1 Cor. 7:32–35).

A study of Jesus's and Paul's comments on celibacy engenders two observations. First, in contrast to the traditional Jewish interpretation of the Old Testament, celibacy is a *positive* concept in the teachings of Jesus and Paul. Whereas in the Old Testament era singleness tended to be viewed negatively, both Jesus and Paul assert, as well as model, the idea that singleness is acceptable, though not the norm (see 1 Cor. 7:9; 1 Tim. 4:1–3). What is more, celibacy is viewed as a *gift* bestowed by God. This clearly was a revolutionary teaching for a first-century audience.

Moreover, in the book of Revelation the seer praises celibacy, at least metaphorically, as he describes the 144,000 end-time Jewish evangelists as those "who have not defiled themselves with women . . . *they are virgins*" (Rev. 14:4–5). Interestingly, the impetus for the celibacy of the 144,000 evangelists is the same as that mentioned by Jesus and Paul—greater devotion to the Lord, or in the words of the seer, to "follow the Lamb wherever he goes." Overall, then, celibacy is viewed positively in the New Testament from the Gospels to Revelation.

A second observation that arises from a reading of Jesus's and Paul's statements on singleness is that not only is celibacy a divine gift, but it is also a divine calling that is both limited to the select *few* and freely *chosen* rather than foisted upon the individual by his or her circumstances or condition. As Jesus said, "Not everyone can receive this saying, but only those to whom it is given. . . . Let the one who is able to receive this receive it" (Matt. 19:11–12). Jesus's words seem to indicate that it takes special grace from God for individuals called to celibacy for the sake of God's kingdom to recognize this calling.

The apostle Paul, writing to the Corinthians, casts the issue as follows: "But because of the temptation to sexual immorality, each man should have his own wife and each woman her own husband. . . . *But if they cannot exercise self-control*, they should marry. For it is better to marry than to burn with passion. . . . But if you do marry, you have not sinned" (1 Cor. 7:2, 9, 28). Clearly, then, while singleness is a positive condition in which Christians are free to remain if they are unmarried, especially if they are so gifted, it is wrong to expect people to adopt a life of singleness against their will. Indeed, as Paul later wrote to Timothy, forbidding marriage is one of the "teachings of demons" (see 1 Tim. 4:1–3).

Third, our understanding of Paul's teaching on singleness hinges largely on our *reconstruction of the Corinthian context* in which Paul formulated his pronouncements in 1 Corinthians 7. The recent consensus is that 1 Corinthians 7:1–7 should be read as Paul's response to those in Corinth who advocated the cessation of sexual relations in marriage for ostensibly ascetic purposes. If so, 1 Corinthians 7:1b, "It is good for a man not to have sexual relations with a woman," is a direct quotation from the Corinthian letter, and the fundamental issue the Corinthians are raising to

Paul has to do with sexual relations *in marriage* rather than the question of whether or not a person should get married at all.

However, it is certainly possible that the message of the text also includes the notion that we should genuinely encourage our congregations to consider the calling and *charisma* of singleness as something truly good (i.e., "You can remain as you are"), while at the same time fully reassuring those who do not feel comfortable with the calling of singleness that God's provision of marriage is not a moral compromise but is his excellent and noble provision for the majority who are gifted otherwise.[10] What is clear in 1 Corinthians 7:1–7, then, is that God calls us all to a high (i.e., morally chaste) view of both singleness and marriage.

TOWARD A BIBLICAL THEOLOGY OF SINGLENESS

The question arises, why does the biblical treatment of singleness show the remarkable degree of development that was demonstrated above? As Barry Danylak shows, procreation was an integral part of the Old Testament covenants, starting with God's covenant with Abraham (Gen. 12:1–9; 15:1–21; 18:1–15; 22:15–19) and continuing through the Davidic covenant (2 Sam. 7:12–13).[11] The entire family inheritance structure in Old Testament times was predicated upon the centrality of the offspring-blessing relationship (Ex. 32:13; Deut. 4:20; 32:9; 1 Kings 21:3; 1 Chron. 28:8), and levirate marriage provides for the continuation of the family name (Ruth).

Remarkably, however, in Isaiah and the Prophets we begin to see "hints of a new paradigm of fulfillment of the Abrahamic blessings."[12] In the third "Servant Song" of Isaiah, we read that while the suffering servant would be "cut off out of the land of the living" (Isa. 53:8), he would nonetheless "see his offspring" (Isa. 53:10). Thus the new blessings come not through physical offspring but through offspring raised up by God himself. This supernatural birth is made possible through the vicarious sacrifice of the servant of the Lord. Strikingly, the following chapter in Isaiah begins with the song of the barren woman who rejoices that "the children of the desolate one will be more than the children of her who is married" (Isa. 54:1).

What is more, in Isaiah 56 we find another portrait of restoration, this time not for the barren woman but for the eunuch. The eunuch, who because of his physical defects had been cut off from the Lord's assembly (Deut. 23:1) now is granted access to the restored temple (Isa. 56:3–5). He who was a dry tree without children (v. 3) now is given "a name better than sons and daughters," "an everlasting name that shall not be cut off" (v. 5). In fact, "This passage is a reminder for single people and those without children that the legacy they have as a member of God's eternal house is something far superior to any physical legacy that children and offspring can provide. God himself is their portion and inheritance (Lam 3:24; Ezek 44:28)."[13]

The Isaianic theme of offspring and the new covenant it represents resurfaces prominently in the New Testament.[14] In Galatians 3, Paul makes clear that God's covenant blessings are to be enjoyed in Christ through faith by his spiritual offspring, the children of promise. In Romans 9, Paul adds that membership in the covenant is not merely a result of being a physical descendant of Abraham but a matter of being a spiritual offspring through faith in Christ (see esp. Rom. 9:6, 8). Elsewhere in the New Testament, "inheritance" language is applied to spiritual rather than natural offspring (e.g., Eph. 1:14, 18; 5:5; 1 Pet. 1:3–4).

With regard to Jesus's life and teaching, his message to Nicodemus focused on the necessity of a new, spiritual birth, even for Jews (John 3:3, 5). In other parts of the Gospels, Jesus repeatedly emphasized the spiritual nature of those who would be included among his followers and in his family in contrast to natural flesh-and-blood ties (e.g., Matt. 12:46–50; Luke 14:26; 18:28–30). While not undermining the traditional family structure, Jesus did elevate the kingdom of God as of supreme significance that demanded from his followers a loyalty that exceeded even that required by one's natural family. Jesus also taught that there would be no marriage in heaven (Matt. 22:30; Mark 12:25; Luke 20:35).

In Matthew 19:11–12, Jesus speaks of three classes of eunuchs: those who are eunuchs by birth (congenital defect), those who were eunuchs made by men (physical castration), and those who made themselves eunuchs for the sake of the kingdom of heaven. Jesus's use of "eunuch" language may be surprising at first, owing to the disdain directed toward eunuchs in contemporary Jewish culture. At a second glance, however, eunuchs provided a fitting model for the point Jesus was trying to make. Since they were childless, they could offer devoted, undistracted service to the king. While not for everyone (Matt. 19:11), Jesus encouraged those who were able to receive his teaching to do so (Matt. 19:12). Paul's teaching is in a similar vein (1 Cor. 7:32, 35).

A study of Jesus's life further reveals that although he was unmarried, he did not live alone. His inner circle was made up of three of his followers, and he was accompanied by the twelve apostles as well as a group of devoted women followers (Luke 8:1–3). Jesus also maintained close friendships with others, perhaps most notably the family of Lazarus, Martha, and Mary in Bethany near Jerusalem (Luke 10:38–42; John 11:1–12:19). As an itinerant preacher, Jesus enjoyed the hospitality of others and came in close contact with many who had need and ministered to them. When at last he gathered, as the paternal head, with his followers prior to his death at the Last Supper to institute the new covenant, he left a legacy to his spiritual offspring and presided over the new family of God, which he brought into being through his sacrificial death. In these and other ways Jesus serves as a model of one who dedicated himself to service in God's kingdom.[15]

How, then, are we to account for the change in the presentation of singleness from the Old Testament to the New? As Danylak explains, "The significance of singleness changes from the Old Testament context to the New Testament context in light of the intrinsic differences between the old and new covenants they largely reflect."[16] While physical offspring was vital to the fulfillment of the old covenant, the new covenant is built on the notion of the production of spiritual offspring through the vicarious sacrifice of the suffering servant of the Lord. Jesus's life, for its part, serves as a paradigm of dedicated kingdom service for those who are called and choose to be "eunuchs for the sake of the kingdom of heaven."

What, then, are the implications of the biblical teaching on singleness for the church today? As Danylak notes, singleness serves as "a reminder that the entrance to the people of God is through spiritual rebirth rather than physical family membership. Likewise, the presence of both single and married people in the church together signifies the fact that the church lives between the ages. Married people are necessary because the church is still part of the current age, but single people remind it that the spiritual age has already been inaugurated in Christ and awaits imminent consummation."[17] It is incumbent upon the church to encourage the kind of communal and congregational life that recognizes and lives out these spiritual realities.

ISSUES INVOLVING SINGLENESS
Singleness and Ministry
Applied to the contemporary context, singleness should be recognized as a gift for the select few that holds significant *advantages for ministry* but is neither *intrinsically superior* nor *inferior* to the institution of marriage. While Paul assumes that church officers as a rule will be married (1 Tim. 3:2, 12; Titus 1:6) and considers marriage and the family to be a training and proving ground for prospective church leaders (1 Tim. 3:4–5; see 1 Tim. 3:15), this should not be construed as a requirement. The church needs both its single and its married members. While in most churches married couples with children make up the fabric of the congregation, married

people should treat single people as full and rightful members of their congregation.

Cohabitation and Premarital Sex

As we have argued, Scripture presents marriage as a sacred, inviolable, and exclusive relationship between one man and one woman, properly entered into by the mutual pledge of lifelong marital faithfulness and consummated by sexual relations, which constitutes the marriage as a "one-flesh" union (Gen. 2:23–24). According to Jesus, the marital union constitutes the man and the woman as no longer two but one, having been joined together by none other than God (Matt. 19:6; Mark 10:8–9). Paul maintains that even sexual intercourse with a prostitute results in a one-flesh union, albeit an illegitimate one (1 Cor. 6:15–17, referring to Gen. 2:24; see Eph. 5:31). The same is true for any form of sexual intercourse outside of a monogamous marriage relationship. While it is inevitable that those in the larger culture who are not committed to observing biblical teaching in this area persist in cohabitation or engage in illicit sex, there can be no doubt that this is not an option for believers. *Sexual abstinence prior to marriage* and *sexual faithfulness in marriage* are the biblical expectations, and it is evident that the practice of the former constitutes the best preparation for the observance of the latter.

What, then, are the implications for Christians who engage in cohabitation and premarital sex, be it out of ignorance regarding the biblical teaching on this issue or in deliberate, conscious violation of Scripture? And what are the implications for unbelievers who live together without being married and/or practice premarital or extramarital sex? In the case of genuine believers, if they are members of a local church, those in leadership ought to instruct the young people that Scripture does not permit cohabitation and premarital sex and exhort them to stop sinning against the Lord in this way. If the exhortation goes unheeded, church discipline ought to be exercised.

In the case of unbelievers, their primary need is turning away from their sin and trusting Christ as their Lord and Savior, which transcends the issue of cohabitation and premarital sex.

Courtship and Dating

Contemporary Western culture has come a long way from the arranged marriages of ancient Israel. Yet as a result of this pendulum shift often parents have virtually no say in whom their son or daughter chooses to marry (though parents are often still expected to pay for their daughter's wedding). One of the key issues in this area is what constitutes true love. Young people often say that they have no control over whom they "fall in love" with, and Hollywood has done its fair share to perpetrate the stereotype that love has a pull or power over people that is impossible or futile to resist.

Over against this travesty of love, Scripture sets the ideal of human love that is other-centered, self-sacrificial, and focused on the true inner person rather than on changing external characteristics (see esp. 1 Corinthians 13; see Prov. 31:30). This is the love husbands are called to exercise toward their wives, a love that is patterned after Christ's love for the church (Eph. 5:25–30). Not only does the pursuit and exercise of this kind of love make a difference in what one will look for in a mate, but it will also make all the difference in one's marriage relationship. True love will wait to have sex until marriage and will seek to uphold the dignity of the other person.[18]

While we have no direct biblical command dealing with the question (often asked by Christians today) whether dating is appropriate for Christians and, if so, at what age, young men and women certainly should respect their parents' wisdom in setting reasonable parameters in this regard. What is more, they should trust the Lord that in his good time, if he wants them to marry, he will bring their future spouse across their path.

Biblical Teaching on Singleness Addressed to Particular Groups

While Scripture at times addresses the issue of singleness in general, there are other times when it has a specific message to a particular group of single people. The Scriptures have much to say, for example, to young men (and often unmarried). In the Old Testament the book of Proverbs warns young men against falling into the trap of the adulterous woman and exhorts them to guard their hearts in all purity. Examples of fine and godly young single men include Joseph, Samuel, David, Solomon, and Daniel and his friends, to name but a few. In the New Testament, Paul instructs his foremost disciple, Timothy, to cleanse himself from anything dishonorable and to be set apart and useful to his Master, ready for every good work (2 Tim. 2:21). This highlights the spiritual dimension of a young man's life and his potential for service in the church. Young men hold particular promise and potential for good in the kingdom, yet they also have pronounced points of vulnerability, especially in the area of sexual temptation, which Satan will seek to attack to render them ineffective.[19]

Most of the biblical material relating to women is addressed to married women. Scripture's primary emphasis with regard to women (including those who are young) is that of *modesty in appearance* (1 Tim. 2:9–10; 1 Pet. 3:3–6; though self-control is repeatedly mentioned as well: see 1 Tim. 2:9, 15; Titus 2:3, 5). Modesty is not limited to the issue of what kinds of clothes women wear. It extends also to nonverbal cues, mannerisms, suggestive behavior, and acting aggressively and taking improper initiative. Modesty does not mean that women must wear only dull, unfashionable clothes, shunning makeup or perfume, or remaining silent in the company of the opposite sex. Rather, their focus ought to be on developing spiritual virtues and on devoting themselves to good works (1 Tim. 2:9–10).

Another group of unmarried men and women that receives special treatment in Scripture is widows and widowers. According to James, pure religion is this: "To look after orphans and widows in their distress" (James 1:27 NIV).[20] Widows were a recognized group of people among the first Christians (Acts 9:39, 41). The apostle Paul addresses the church's responsibility to provide for "true" widows (1 Tim. 5:3–16, which includes guidelines on identifying widows worthy of support). Younger widows, for their part, ought not to be held to a pledge of singleness that they may not be able to keep—and thus incur judgment—when their sensual desires overcome their devotion to Christ (1 Tim. 5:11–12). Thus Paul's advice to younger widows is to remarry, care for their children, manage their homes—filling out what is referred to merely as "childbearing" in 1 Timothy 2:15—and to give the enemy no opportunity for slander (1 Tim. 5:14; see 2 Cor. 5:12). Paul concludes his instructions concerning widows with an exhortation to believing women to care for widows in their family in order to relieve the church (1 Tim. 5:16). Caring for widows and other needy individuals is one important way in which the church can reflect the gracious heart of God and the compassion and mercy of the Lord Jesus Christ.

Single parents may be divorcees, widows/widowers, or those who had one or several children without marrying their partner. This group is faced with several challenges, including a need to provide for their children materially while being available to nurture them emotionally and spiritually as well as the lack of a spouse, which leaves the children without a primary role model of one sex, be it male or female. Paul's above-cited advice to younger widows would seem to apply also to single parents at large; namely that, if possible, they ought to remarry in order to lighten their load both materially and with regard to their parenting task.[21]

Divorcees are yet another group that makes up the amorphous category of "singles." Believers should come alongside divorcees and offer support and encouragement. The costs of divorce are high, and divorces leave many scars that require healing, both for the divorced person and for any children of divorce.[22] Divorce is not the unpardonable sin, and forgiveness is always available in Christ, even though there will still be consequences with which divorced people will have to cope.

PRACTICAL IMPLICATIONS

What are some of the practical implications of singleness?[23] First, singles (as well as married people) need to keep in mind the fact that *the married state is not the final destiny of anyone* (Matt. 22:30; see Rom. 7:3; 1 Cor. 7:39). This is because as members of the body of Christ, all believers are ultimately betrothed to the Lamb to be with him and to glorify him forever (Isa. 43:7; 1 Cor. 10:31; 2 Cor. 11:2). Second, in view of our ultimate destiny and our current betrothal to Christ, *it is imperative that singles remain content*, for as the apostle Paul wrote, "Godliness with contentment is great gain" (1 Tim. 6:6; see Phil. 4:11). Third, singles ought to remember that all who forsake marriage and family in the present world for the sake of God are in this life *rewarded with new family in the body of Christ*, as well as with an eternal family in the kingdom of heaven (see Luke 18:28–30).

6

HOMOSEXUALITY

When compared with the biblical pattern of marriage and the family set forth in the opening chapters of Genesis, homosexuality falls short on numerous fronts.[1] First, as the *antithesis of heterosexuality*, homosexuality is at odds with God's design for marriage and the family at its most foundational level. This is made clear by the words of Genesis 2:24, which conceive of marriage in heterosexual rather than homosexual terms: "A *man* [masculine] shall leave his father and his mother and hold fast to his *wife* [feminine], and they [the man and the woman] shall become one flesh."

A second component of the biblical model of marriage that homosexuality violates is its *complementary* nature. The marital roles were assigned by God at creation (Gen. 2:18, 20) and were reaffirmed both after the fall (Gen. 3:16–19) and in New Testament teaching (Eph. 5:22–33; 1 Pet. 3:1–7). Since these roles are tied inherently and unalterably to gender, same-sex partners cannot participate in this aspect of biblical marriage.

A third component of God's design for marriage and the family that homosexuality does not fulfill is the *duty to procreate*. This can be seen in the very first commandment ever given by God to the human couple: "Be fruitful and multiply and fill the earth" (Gen. 1:28). By nature, homosexuality falls short of this essential component of the biblical/traditional model of marriage and the family, since it precludes reproduction.

Not only does homosexuality fall short of the biblical pattern of marriage with regard to *heterosexuality, complementarity*, and *fertility*, homosexual couples also often do not uphold other aspects of biblical marriage such as *monogamy, fidelity,* and *durability.* The extent of homosexuality's departure from the biblical model of marriage and the family may be one of the reasons why this sin is so severely chastised in Scripture.

HOMOSEXUALITY IN THE OLD TESTAMENT

While Scripture alludes or explicitly refers to homosexuality at least two dozen times,[2] the three main sections of Scripture dealing with homosexuality are the account of the destruction of Sodom and Gomorrah in Genesis 18–19, the sexual laws of the Holiness Code in Leviticus 18 and 20, and the apostle Paul's remarks on homosexuality in his letter to the Romans and in his first letters to the Corinthians and to Timothy. As will be seen, each of these biblical passages clearly condemns homosexuality, and it is only by a radical reinterpretation that the scriptural message regarding homosexuality is turned into a positive and accepting stance toward this practice.

Sodom and Gomorrah

The account of the destruction of Sodom and Gomorrah (Gen. 18:17–19:29) is probably the best-known episode in Scripture revealing God's opposition to homosexuality. The account is particularly significant for at least the following three reasons: (1) it is both the first and the most detailed account of God's confrontation of homosexuality; (2) it is the only pre-Mosaic mention of homosexuality in Scripture; and (3) the sin and destruction of Sodom and Gomorrah are frequently cited in Scripture—often clearly in the context of sexual sin.[3] It is therefore no wonder that homosexual advocates have devoted considerable attention to this account, for if they can convincingly demonstrate that the transgression that precipitated the ruin of these two cities was not homosexuality, they will have overturned a very important portion of the biblical witness against it.

In the attempt to revise the traditional understanding of the sin of Sodom and Gomorrah, two major new interpretations have been proposed. First, some scholars have suggested that the sin that led to the ruin of these two cities was not homosexuality but rather *gang rape*. Although Walter Barnett was not the first to offer this interpretation, he has been arguably the most influential proponent of this view.[4] Barnett believes that this event, along with the companion account of the Israelite civil war with the Benjamites over the sexual sin of the Gibeonites (Judges 19–21), may not even have entailed *homosexual* gang rape but rather *heterosexual* gang rape.

In response, the sin of Sodom and Gomorrah did indeed involve the *intent to rape*. It is erroneous, however, to limit the transgression of these two cities *exclusively* to gang rape and to redefine the intended sin as a form of heterosexual-oriented rape. Identifying the sin that led to the destruction of Sodom and Gomorrah as heterosexual rape is also contradicted by Jude's statement that the inhabitants of "Sodom and Gomorrah . . . indulged in sexual immorality and *pursued unnatural desire . . . defil[ing] the flesh*" (Jude 6–8; see 2 Pet. 2:4–10). The offenders at Sodom and Gomorrah did not just have *uncontrollable* sexual desires, but *unnatural* sexual desires.

A second, even more influential, attempt at revising the traditional understanding of the sin of Sodom and Gomorrah holds that it was not homosexuality, but rather *inhospitality*. Doubtless the most influential proponent of this view has been D. Sherwin Bailey, who is widely recognized as the first scholar to have suggested this interpretation.[5] This view rests upon the definition of the Hebrew word *yāda'* which is translated as "know" in Genesis 19:5. According to this interpretation, since in the vast majority of the 943 uses of this word in the Old Testament it means "to get acquainted with," this ought to be its connotation in the account of Sodom and Gomorrah. Therefore, when the men of Sodom surrounded Lot's house and inquired, "Where are the men who came to you tonight? Bring them out to us, that we may *know* them"

(Gen. 19:5), they were simply asking to be *introduced* to the angelic visitors because Lot had failed to acquaint them properly with the townspeople.

While this interpretation is creative and persuasive to some, a review of the facts surrounding the destruction of Sodom and Gomorrah reveals that this view, too, is untenable. Concerning the Hebrew word *yāda'*, it must be noted that while this term usually does mean "to get acquainted with," it can also refer to sexual relations, as it clearly does in Genesis 4:1, 17, 25; 24:16; and 38:26. The decisive factor in determining the definition of this word (or any term with multiple possible meanings) must be the context. Following this principle, in the context of the Sodom and Gomorrah passage *yāda'* must have a sexual connotation when it occurs in Genesis 19:5, for when the term recurs three verses later the sexual meaning is the only one that makes sense. Otherwise, Lot would be saying that his daughters, who were engaged to two of the inhabitants of Sodom, had never actually been acquainted with a man! Moreover, Lot's offering of his two daughters to the men of Sodom makes absolutely no sense if the men knocking at his door were merely asking to be introduced to his house guests. Why not just introduce the angels to the inquisitive townspeople if that was all that was requested of him?

While other critiques could be levied against both these arguments, it is highly likely that the sin that brought God's judgment on Sodom and Gomorrah was indeed that of homosexuality.

The Levitical Holiness Code

Two laws in the Holiness Code specifically address homosexuality. These are Leviticus 18:22 ("You shall not lie with a male as with a woman; it is an abomination") and 20:13 ("If a man lies with a male as with a woman, both of them have committed an abomination; they shall surely be put to death; their blood is upon them"). These laws constitute a significant portion of the biblical witness against homosexuality, for they both explicitly address homosexual relations in a casuistic manner and prescribe the death penalty for homosexual offenders (which God had previously enacted at Sodom and Gomorrah).

Pro-homosexual exegetes who have dealt with these verses have generally adopted an occasional, culturally relative approach— that is, they claim that these verses are culture-bound temporal directives given to the Israelites, not eternally binding moral absolutes meant for the elect throughout the ages. While individual interpreters have made this argument in different forms with various nuances, the foundational argument that supports this view is usually the same. In short, this view centers on the use of the Hebrew word *tō'ēbāh*, which is translated "abomination" in both of these verses. According to proponents of this position, when the term *tō'ēbāh* is used in Scripture, it usually refers to some type of ritual impurity connected to idol worship. Therefore, when God prohibited homosexuality in Leviticus 18:22 and 20:13, he was not addressing homosexuality as such but rather, in the context of this portion of the Holiness Code, prohibiting *homosexual acts performed by Canaanite temple prostitutes as part of the worship of false gods.*

In response to this interpretation, it must be noted that while the Hebrew word *tō'ēbāh* can refer to some type of ritual impurity connected to idol worship (see 2 Kings 16:3; Isa. 44:19; Jer. 16:18; Ezek. 7:20), it frequently does not have this connotation (see Gen. 43:32; Ps. 88:8; Prov. 6:16–19; 28:9). In fact, sometimes *tō'ēbāh* refers to activities that are morally offensive to God, such as homosexuality. In the context of this passage in the Holiness Code, it is interesting to note that activities other than homosexuality are also labeled as *tō'ēbāh* (see Lev. 18:26), including incest (Lev. 18:6–18), adultery (Lev. 18:20), and bestiality (Lev. 18:23). If we were to apply a consistent hermeneutic throughout this passage, we would be forced to conclude that these other activities are likewise only prohibited within the context of idol worship. Yet such an interpretation would be untenable in light of the fact that these other activities are consistently condemned throughout

Scripture, as is homosexuality. Given that homosexuality is prohibited throughout Scripture, it should be noted that *the context
of Scripture's prohibition of a certain activity does not necessarily limit
the immorality of that activity to that particular context.* It seems clear,
therefore, that the sin prohibited in these two verses must be
understood, as it traditionally has been, to be the general practice
of homosexuality.

HOMOSEXUALITY IN THE NEW TESTAMENT

Our major source concerning the New Testament's view of homosexuality is the apostle Paul, who refers to homosexuality in his
letter to the Romans and in his first letters to the Corinthians and
Timothy.[6]

The Letter to the Romans

The major passage on homosexuality in Paul's writings is found in
the first chapter of his letter to the Romans, where his denunciation of homosexuality is part of his larger presentation of the universal sinfulness of humanity in its rejection of God the Creator
(Rom. 1:18–23). Because of this rejection, Paul contends, God gave
depraved humanity over "in the lusts of their hearts to impurity,
to the dishonoring of their bodies among themselves, because
they exchanged the truth about God for a lie and worshiped and
served the creature rather than the Creator" (Rom. 1:24–25).

In what follows Paul elaborates on precisely what he means
by "the dishonoring of their bodies among themselves": "For this
reason God gave them up to dishonorable passions. For their
women exchanged natural relations for those that are contrary
to nature; and the men likewise gave up natural relations with
women and were consumed with passion for one another, men
committing shameless acts with men and receiving in themselves
the due penalty for their error" (Rom. 1:26–27).

Paul proceeds to reiterate that these "shameless acts" are a
result of people's rejection of God, who consequently "gave them

up to a debased mind to do what ought not to be done" (Rom. 1:28). This is followed by a vice list, in which homosexuality is associated with a long litany of sinful human attitudes and behaviors (Rom. 1:29–31; see 1 Cor. 6:9–10; 1 Tim. 1:9–10). Paul closes this section by issuing the indictment that though these people "know God's righteous decree that those who practice such things deserve to die, they not only do them but give approval to those who practice them" (Rom. 1:32). Thus God's judgment is pronounced not only on practicing homosexuals but also on those who condone such behavior (see 1 Cor. 5:1–13).

It is probably no coincidence that it is in Paul's letter to the Romans that this sweeping indictment of human depravity, including a stern denunciation of homosexuality (as well as lesbianism, Rom. 1:26), is found. At the time of writing (c. AD 57), the Roman world was known for its moral debauchery, sexual excess, and perversity.[7] The rule of Claudius (AD 41–54) is notorious for such evils, as is that of his successor, Nero (AD 54–68), during whose reign Paul penned his letter to the Romans. A few decades later, the book of Revelation depicts the Roman Empire as the "whore Babylon," of whose "wine of the passion of her sexual immorality" all nations have drunk (Rev. 18:3; see Rev. 17:4–6; 18:9; 19:2).

In light of the literary and cultural context of Paul's reference to homosexuality in the first chapter of Romans, there seems little doubt that he considered homosexuality at large, rather than merely more narrowly defined aberrant subsets of homosexual behavior, to be contrary to God's created order and hence worthy of condemnation. What is more, Paul condemns not only those who *engage* in homosexual behavior but also those who *condone* such behavior without themselves engaging in it. However, recently attempts have been made to identify the sin condemned in Romans and other New Testament writings as a more narrow offense. Since these efforts often take their point of departure at the specific Greek word *arsenokoitēs*, which does not occur in

Romans but is found in Paul's two other references to the subject, we will deal with these objections below.

First Corinthians

While Paul's denunciation of homosexuality in his letter to the Romans involves his use of various circumlocutions of the practice ("dishonoring of their bodies among themselves," Rom. 1:24; "exchanged natural relations for those that are contrary to nature," Rom. 1:26; "gave up natural relations," "consumed with passion for one another," "men committing shameless acts with men," Rom. 1:27), he employs the Greek term *arsenokoitēs* to refer to homosexuality in his other two major references to the subject, 1 Corinthians 6:9 and 1 Timothy 1:10 (in 1 Cor. 6:9, the term *malakos* is used as well).

It should be noted at the outset that first-century Corinth was notorious for its sexual immorality. Likewise, Paul's reference to homosexuals in his first letter to the Corinthians is part of a section in which he deals with a variety of sin issues confronting the Corinthian church, most of which were sexual in nature. After chastising the Corinthians, Paul asserts that "neither the sexually immoral, nor idolaters, nor adulterers, nor men who practice homosexuality [note: the original has two Greek words, possibly referring to both the passive and active partners in homosexual intercourse], nor thieves, nor the greedy, nor drunkards, nor revilers, nor swindlers will inherit the kingdom of God" (1 Cor. 6:9–10; see 1 Cor. 5:10). Paul adds, "And such were some of you. But you were washed, you were sanctified, you were justified in the name of the Lord Jesus Christ and by the Spirit of our God" (1 Cor. 6:11). In the following section Paul denounces Christians who have sex with prostitutes, contending that this is a gross misrepresentation of true Christian freedom and urging believers to flee from sexual immorality (1 Cor. 6:12–20).

The vice list in 1 Corinthians 6:9–10, of which the two terms related to homosexuality are a part, expands the list in 5:10 by repeating all six items found in the antecedent passage.[8] In fact, the earlier list frames the subsequent one in that the first two and the last four items are repeated, with the four added characteristics being placed at the center. The terms "sexually immoral" and "idolaters" reflect the two major issues addressed in the context, sexual immorality (see 1 Cor. 5:1–13; 6:12–20) and idolatry (see 1 Cor. 8:1–11:1). Of the four new items, three (adulterers, *malakoi*, and *arsenokoitai*) are sexual; the fourth is thieves (though "robbers" may be more accurate). The vice list concludes with the four other items from 1 Corinthians 5:10–11.

Looking at the three items relevant for our present purposes, "adulterers" (*moikoi*) bears the straightforward meaning of married persons having sexual relations outside marriage (Ex. 20:14; Lev. 20:10; Deut. 5:18; see Luke 18:11). The next two terms, *malakoi* and *arsenokoitai*, require more extended comment. Both expressions have to do with homosexuality and are at times conflated into one English phrase in translation, such as the ESV's "men who practice homosexuality" or the NIV's "men who have sex with men." The first term, *malakos*, means literally "soft" (see Matt. 11:8 = Luke 7:25) and in Paul's day served as an epithet for the "soft" or effeminate (i.e., passive) partner in a homosexual (pederastic) relationship. Importantly, *malakoi* (as well as *arsenokoitai*) refers to behavior and not mere orientation, as is implied by Paul's comment in 1 Corinthians 6:11, "And such were some of you."

It has been argued, however, that the New Testament references ought to be restricted only to an aberrant subset of homosexual behavior, whether (1) homosexual prostitution,[9] (2) pederasty,[10] (3) homosexual acts but not "celibate" homosexual relationships,[11] or (4) some negative, dehumanizing, and exploitive form of homosexual relationships but not to homosexuality in general.[12] Others object (5) that the concept of homosexuality has changed, so that using the term in modern translations of *arsenokoitai* is misleading.[13] However, any attempt to limit the New Testament references to homosexuality to a narrower subset of aberrant homosexual behavior must be judged unconvincing, and the traditional view must be upheld that the New Testament, as does the Old Testament, condemns homosexuality as sin and incompatible with God's created order.

To this overall conclusion regarding homosexuality we may add several observations that flow from our study of 1 Corinthians 6:9–10 in particular:

1. The church is told *not to tolerate sexual immorality in its midst* (1 Cor. 5:1–13). This includes those who practice homosexuality. It seems clear that the apostle Paul would not have tolerated openly practicing homosexuals as members (much less in leadership) of a Christian congregation.

2. Homosexuality is *listed together with many other vices* as an attribute that will bar entrance into God's kingdom (1 Cor. 6:9–11; see 1 Cor. 5:10). If homosexuality is not acceptable in heaven, the church must be clear that it is not acceptable in the church either.

3. Paul makes clear that some of the members of the Corinthian church were *former homosexuals* (1 Cor. 6:11). This shows that true transformation of homosexuals is possible in Christ. As Paul notes, those individuals were cleansed from their sin ("washed," perhaps referring to spiritual regeneration, with possible secondary reference to baptism), set apart for God and his service ("sanctified"), and acquitted and made right with God ("justified") in Christ and by the Spirit (1 Cor. 6:11; see 1 Cor. 1:30). This is a hopeful note indeed for any homosexuals who are willing to repent of their sin and appropriate Christ's forgiveness and life-transforming power.

First Timothy

The final significant reference to homosexuality, in 1 Timothy, like that in 1 Corinthians, is included in a vice list. The reference is part of a digression (1 Tim. 1:8–11) that elaborates on the nature of the heretics' misuse of the law. This is followed by a second digression (1 Tim. 1:12–17) that presents Paul, in contrast to the false teachers, as the model of a sinner saved by grace. This makes clear that Paul is not exalting himself above his opponents because he is intrinsically superior to them. Rather, it is solely his acceptance of God's gracious offer of salvation and forgiveness in Christ that sets him apart from the heretics.

The vices (or sinners), listed here in six groups of two (or three), plus a concluding catchall phrase, are as follows:

1. lawbreakers and rebels;
2. ungodly and sinful;
3. unholy and irreligious (jointly echoing the first four commandments);
4. those who kill their fathers or mothers, murderers (echoing the fifth and sixth commandments, "Honor your father and your mother" and "You shall not murder");
5. adulterers and homosexuals (echoing the seventh commandment, "You shall not commit adultery");
6. slave traders or kidnappers, liars, and perjurers (echoing the eighth and ninth commandments, "You shall not steal" and "You shall not give false testimony against your neighbor"); and whatever else is contrary to sound doctrine.

Within these pairs (or expressions of three), the offenses cited fall roughly within the same category. Most relevant for our present purposes, both "adulterers" (*pornois*; see 1 Cor. 6:9: *pornoi, moikoi*) and "homosexuals" (*arsenokoitais*) refer to sexual sins that constitute a violation of the seventh commandment. It appears that Paul's list, after three general pairs (conveying the notion of godlessness, which may in some general sense be related to the first four commandments), follows the second portion of the Ten Commandments (Ex. 20:12–16; Deut. 5:16–20), specifically commandments five through nine. Strong terms are chosen, perhaps to highlight the degree of evil in the pagan world and the need of law for those who have not heard the gospel (see Rom. 1:21–32).

The list of wrongdoers in 1 Timothy 1:9–10 leads Paul to

discuss the "grace of our Lord" Christ Jesus coming into the world "to save sinners" (1 Tim. 1:14–15). Paul himself was once in the category of those whose actions were condemned by the law; now he has been shown mercy. This holds out hope even for the false teachers and those guilty of violating any of the above-mentioned commandments—but only if they repent and desist from their improper use of the Mosaic law.

Once again, then, Paul includes homosexuality in a vice list (though he does not here distinguish between the two partners in homosexual intercourse, as he does in 1 Cor. 9–10), in the present instance subsuming homosexuality together with adultery as a violation of the seventh commandment and hence indicating its unacceptability for Christians.

PRACTICAL IMPLICATIONS

The biblical verdict on homosexuality is consistent. From Genesis to Revelation, from Jesus to Paul, from Romans to the Pastorals, Scripture with one voice affirms that homosexuality is sin and a moral offense to God. The contemporary church corporately, and biblical Christians individually, must bear witness to the unanimous testimony of Scripture unequivocally and fearlessly.

But what are the practical implications of the Bible's unified witness against homosexuality? At the outset, we must be clear that the visible church ought to continue to oppose this distortion of the Creator's biblical/traditional model of marriage and family. Denominations that have departed from Christendom's historically orthodox position on homosexuality (either by openly endorsing homosexuality or by remaining silent on the issue) are certainly not in step with Judeo-Christian tradition nor, more importantly, with the Word of God.

Yet, for those who are in churches that oppose homosexuality or for Christians who are just personally convinced of the sinfulness of this practice, a more personal dilemma may surface. What do you do if a friend or family member is involved in homosexuality, or if you are homosexual yourself? While this may seem like a daunting problem, especially for those directly involved, we should remember that, as for virtually every other transgression mentioned in the Bible, 1 John 1:9 applies: "If we confess our sins, he is faithful and just to forgive us our sins and to cleanse us from all unrighteousness." Homosexuality, then, is not the unpardonable sin, and forgiveness is available (1 Cor. 6:11). Yet forgiveness implies repentance, and repentance implies admission of wrong. The church would fail in its scriptural mandate if it were exercising tolerance *apart from* repentance and acceptance *apart from* admission of wrong (see 1 Corinthians 5).

Clearly, then, homosexuality is a sin that can be overcome. Fortunately, a number of ministries and other resources are available for those who are trying to break away from homosexuality.[14]

DIVORCE AND REMARRIAGE

While the beauty of God's plan for marriage is plainly laid out in Scripture and many long to experience the kind of intimacy and love found only in biblical marriage, the sad reality is that marriage relationships are often broken and fall short of the biblical ideal. The Scriptures both describe and address this reality while continuing to uphold lifelong monogamous marriage as the ideal.

DIVORCE AND REMARRIAGE IN THE OLD TESTAMENT

Deuteronomy 24:1–4 featured prominently in Jesus's debate with the Pharisees on the subject of divorce and remarriage. As Jesus made clear, this passage should not be construed as a divine endorsement of the practice of divorce and remarriage; rather, it represents an effort to regulate and mitigate existing practices (Matt. 19:8; Mark 10:5).[1] The critical phrase in the legal stipulations that led to extensive rabbinic debate is the expression *'erwat dābār*, which is commonly translated "some indecency" or "something indecent" (Deut. 24:1 NIV).

In Jesus's day, rabbinic schools lined up behind two major interpretive traditions. The conservative school of Shammai (c. 50 BC–AD 30) understood *'erwat dābār* to be a synonym of *dᶜbar 'erwāh*, "a matter of nakedness," and therefore interpreted the phrase to be a reference to immodest behavior or sexual immorality (whether before or after marriage). The more moderate school of Hillel (c. 110–10 BC), however, separated 'erwat, "nakedness," and dābār, "something" (see LXX: "shameful thing"), and, focusing on the earlier words in Deuteronomy 24:1, "finds no favor in his eyes," maintained that divorce was allowed in any instance where a wife had done something displeasing to her husband. This more permissive interpretation seems to have held sway among most of Jesus's contemporaries (see Matt. 19:3).

While there is debate over the meaning of 'erwat dābār today, as in biblical times, one thing that is clear is that in its original context the phrase was not needed or meant to address the issue of divorce in the case of adultery, for, according to the Pentateuch, adultery was punishable by death, not divorce (Lev. 20:10; Deut. 22:22). At the same time, however, since marriage was held in high esteem in ancient Israel, divorce was surely not merely trivial but substantial. As such, Moses's stipulations must not be construed as condoning such divorces but merely as regulating them. The thrust of Deuteronomy 24:1–4 is therefore *descriptive* rather than *prescriptive*, and this seems to be one thing Jesus's contemporaries had misconstrued.[2]

As the passage continues, if a man chooses to divorce his wife and she remarries, he may not take her back in the event of the woman's second divorce or her second husband's death (Deut. 24:2–4). This would be "an abomination before the LORD" (Deut. 24:4). The stipulation serves as a warning to the husband not to divorce too quickly. If he does, and the woman remains unmarried, he can still have her back (see Hosea 3). Once the woman remarries, however, this option is no longer available.

DIVORCE AND REMARRIAGE IN THE NEW TESTAMENT

Given the pressing nature of divorce and remarriage in the modern context, it is perhaps surprising for many contemporary readers to learn that the topic does not dominate the pages of the New Testament. Indeed, the subject of divorce and remarriage is completely absent from the writings of such key New Testament figures as the apostles John and Peter as well as the books authored by Jesus's half-brothers, James and Jude. In fact, the body of material on divorce and remarriage in the New Testament is limited to just two places: some fairly brief pronouncements of Jesus that are recorded in the Gospels (Matt. 5:31–32; 19:3–10; Mark 10:2–12; Luke 16:18) and two occasions in Paul's letters (Rom. 7:1–4; 1 Cor. 7:10–16, 39).

Jesus's Teaching on Divorce and Remarriage
As mentioned, despite the fact that the Mosaic law included pro-visions regulating divorce, the Old Testament makes it clear that divorce falls short of God's ideal (Mal. 2:16). It is not surprising, then, that when asked about divorce and remarriage, Jesus took his listeners all the way back to the beginning, reminding them that God created humanity as male and female (Gen. 1:27) and stipulated that the man, upon marriage, was to leave his father and mother and to be united to his wife (Gen. 2:24) in a one-flesh union before God that people ought not to break: "So they are no longer *two* but *one* flesh. What therefore God has joined together, let not man separate" (Matt. 19:4–6; Mark 10:8–9).

The response of Jesus's audience makes clear that they thought the Mosaic stipulations had in effect superseded God's original purposes at creation. After all, given the theological milieu of the day, in their thinking, why else would divorce have been regulated in Mosaic law (Deut. 24:1–4)? According to Jesus, however, the Mosaic statutes were interposed not to replace the Creator's origi-nal intent but merely in recognition of the reality of human hard-ness of heart (Matt. 19:7–8; Mark 10:5; see Matt. 5:31–32). In fact, marriage was *intended as a lifelong, faithful union of a man and a woman.*

The Disciples' Reaction
Recognizing the high standard set by Jesus, his original followers respond, finding his view unduly restrictive, "If such is the case . . . it is better not to marry" (Matt. 19:10). Jesus, brushing aside

their objection, replies that while a few may indeed have the gift of celibacy (19:11–12), God's original ideal for marriage still stands. Some argue that the disciples' response proves that Jesus's standard must have been even stricter than Shammai's "divorce on the grounds of adultery" view; the disciples' reaction proves that Jesus advocated a "no divorce once the marriage has been consummated" position.[3]

Yet the above arguments remain largely inconclusive, especially since the disciples' reaction was surely influenced by their context and presuppositions. Like many of their Jewish contemporaries, Jesus's followers may have assumed a somewhat more lenient standard—perhaps they even assumed that Jesus's standard was more lenient based upon his compassionate treatment of the adulterous woman mentioned in John 7:53–8:11—and consequently were reacting against Jesus's severe-sounding pronouncement. Also, while contemporary Judaism *required* divorce in the case of sexual immorality, the text seems to indicate that Jesus merely *permitted* it (thus implying the need to forgive). That Jesus's standard regarding divorce was higher even than that of the conservative school of Shammai may therefore adequately account for the disciples' horrified reaction to Jesus's teaching in Matthew 19.[4]

The "Exception Clause"

Much discussion has centered on the one ostensible exception made by Jesus in which case divorce may be permissible. This exception, mentioned in both Matthew 5:32 and 19:9, stipulates that divorce is illegitimate "except for marital unfaithfulness" (NIV 1984) or "sexual immorality" (ESV; ISV; NKJV; HCSB; TNIV; NIV). The parallels in Mark 10:11–12 and Luke 16:18 do not mention the exception, which has led some to argue that Jesus never actually made the exception but that Matthew (or someone else) added it at a later point. Even if this were the case, however (which is unlikely), the "exception clause" would still be part of inerrant, inspired Scripture and thus authoritative for Christians today.

Of those who maintain that Jesus did utter the exception, some endeavor to bring the Matthean exception clause into conformity with the absolute statements in Mark, Luke, and Paul by contending that those passages, rather than Matthew, ought to be the ultimate point of reference. Others are reluctant to subsume the Matthean exception clause too quickly under the absolute statement found in Mark, Luke, and Paul, and argue that both sets of passages ought to be studied in their own right to appreciate Jesus's teaching on the issue at hand.

The incident recorded in Matthew 19:3–12 takes its point of departure from the Pharisees' question, "Is it lawful to divorce one's wife *for any cause?*" (NIV: "for any and every reason"; Matt. 19:3; see Matt. 5:31).[5] As at other occasions, Jesus's opponents seek to involve him in contradiction or otherwise present him with the apparent dilemma of choosing between opposing viewpoints. Indeed, it seems that the phrase "tested him" in Matthew 19:3 (see Mark 10:2) indicates that the religious leaders were trying to get Jesus to choose between competing theological schools as well as to put Jesus in jeopardy with Herod Antipas, just as John the Baptist had suffered for his denunciation of Herod's illicit union with Herodias, his brother Philip's wife (see Matt. 4:12; 11:2–3; 14:3–4; Mark 6:14–29).[6]

The Pharisees' question, then, brings into play the views held by the different rabbinic schools in Jesus's day, as discussed above. Assuming that Jesus himself uttered the "exception clause," how does Jesus align himself with or differ from the rabbinic schools of his day? Clearly, Jesus's view was infinitely stricter than that advocated by the school of Hillel, which held that divorce was permissible "for any cause" (see Matt. 19:3). On the surface at least, Jesus's view is much closer to that of the school of Shammai, which restricted legitimate divorce (with the possibility of remarriage) to marital unfaithfulness. However, as was previously discussed in conjunction with the disciples' reaction to Jesus's teaching, in contrast to Shammai, it seems that Jesus only *permitted* divorce in the case of *porneia* while first-century Judaism *required* it.[7]

What is more, in a very important sense, Jesus's reply transcends the legalistic squabbles between those two rabbinic schools and goes to the very heart of the matter. Essentially, Jesus, in good rabbinic style, shifts the Old Testament warrant from one given passage (Deut. 24:1–4) to an earlier set of passages (Gen. 1:27; 2:24) and hence relativizes the (chronologically) later reference as merely a concession that in no way mitigates the abiding principle established by the foundational texts. Thus, by focusing on the original design of marriage in God's plan, Jesus teaches his followers the true meaning of marriage. Not only does he stress the permanence of marriage as a divine rather than merely human institution, but he contends that divorce is fundamentally at odds with God's purpose in creation.

In fact, Jesus's application of the same standard regarding divorce and remarriage to *both men and women* (see esp. Mark 10:11–12) is nothing less than revolutionary. Despite regulations in the Mosaic law that stipulated equal treatment of men and women with regard to divorce (Lev. 20:10–12), in Old Testament times a double standard prevailed according to which women were required to be faithful to their husbands (or punishment ensued) while the standards for men were considerably more lenient. In Jesus's teaching, however, conjugal rights were set on an equal footing. Thus Jesus taught that lust for other women in a man's heart already constituted adultery (Matt. 5:28), which implies that extramarital affairs are equally wrong for men and women.[8]

Competing Views

In light of the above discussion, it becomes evident that the key issue in understanding Jesus's teaching on divorce and remarriage is the meaning of the term *porneia*, for this is the pivotal term in the "exception clause" uttered by Jesus. There is no universal agreement among Bible-believing Christians as to the exact meaning of *porneia*, yet the suggestions offered by scholars can easily be grouped into one of three competing views.

The first view understands *porneia* to be a reference to adultery/sexual immorality and espouses the *biblical legitimacy of divorce and remarriage for the innocent party of a spouse's adultery/sexual immorality* ("divorce and remarriage"). The second view understands *porneia* to be a reference to some type of sexual sin such as adultery yet holds that while Jesus allowed for *divorce on account of sexual sin, he did not permit remarriage* ("divorce, but no remarriage"). A third view of the exception clause allows for *neither divorce nor remarriage* in the modern context ("no divorce, no remarriage"). Scholars who hold this position understand *porneia* to be a reference to some type of sexual sin that would have made marriage unlawful under Jewish civil law. It should be noted, however, that with all three views mentioned above, there are many nuances and variations within each position.

Suggested Parameters

Given the introductory nature of this volume, rather than championing a particular position in response to the above views, we would like to suggest several parameters for shaping one's view of Jesus's teaching on divorce and remarriage. First, it is important to affirm that the word *porneia* is a general term for sexual sin. The exact meaning of *porneia* is always informed by the context in which the word occurs; yet the term *porneia always refers specifically to sexual sin*. We draw attention to this fact in order to make the point that one cannot derive a doctrine of nonsexual "no fault" divorce from Jesus's use of the word *porneia*.

Second, given the divine design of the institution of marriage, the Old Testament teaching on divorce and remarriage, and the unambiguous portions of Jesus's teaching on the topic, whatever one's view of the "exception clause" may be, it must encourage the sacredness of the marriage bond. That is to say, even if one allows for divorce and remarriage on account of sexual sin (such as adultery, which is the majority view of the modern church), divorce must still be viewed as a result of sin and, consequently, a regrettable failure of God's creation design.

Third, given the pressing nature of divorce and remarriage in contemporary culture, believers ought to take special care to make sure that their respective views are shaped by the biblical text, seeking to avoid common errors such as confusing stringency with holiness or permissiveness with grace. Moreover, in light of the disagreement among orthodox believers over this subject, we encourage all to hold their views of divorce and remarriage charitably, yet with conviction, being open to honest dialogue with those who espouse differing positions.

Paul's Teaching on Divorce and Remarriage

Apart from Jesus's teachings on divorce and remarriage in the Gospels, the only other material on the topic in the New Testament appears in the apostle Paul's letters (Rom. 7:1–4; 1 Cor. 7:10–16, 39). Moreover, Paul's appeal to divorce and remarriage in his letter to the Romans is largely illustrative, and his comments on the topic in writing to the Corinthians appear to be in response to inquiries posed to him by the Corinthian church (see 1 Cor. 7:1).

Romans 7:1–4

In the book of Romans, after demonstrating that all people are condemned (Rom. 1:1–3:20) and explaining the provision of God's righteousness for believers (Rom. 3:21–5:21), beginning in Romans 6:1 and running through Romans 8:39 Paul systematically explains the doctrine of sanctification. Perhaps surprisingly, this section of Paul's epistle to the Romans contains one of the most often overlooked passages on divorce and remarriage in the New Testament. In exhorting his readers to sanctification, Paul, in Romans 7:1–4, uses the eminently practical example of marriage to illustrate the necessity and implications of the death of Christ for the sins of mankind.

The apostle's point in appealing to marriage in this context is this: just as the death of a spouse frees one from the bonds of marriage, so the death of Christ frees one from the bonds of sin. Or, more practically speaking, as it relates to sanctification, just as the death of a spouse frees one to marry another, so the death of Christ unites one to Jesus "in order that we may bear fruit for God" (Rom. 7:4).

Such teaching about sanctification by way of an analogy with marriage would have been readily understood by Paul's Jewish and Hellenistic readers, who the apostle says "know the law" (Rom. 7:1), presumably including the creation narrative. While this is true, however, it is important to remember that Paul's point in Romans 7:1–4 was not to give an exhaustive discourse on the morality of divorce and remarriage but rather to illustrate a deeper truth regarding the necessity and implications of the atonement.

1 Corinthians 7:10–16, 39

The final passage on the subject of divorce and remarriage in the New Testament is found in 1 Corinthians 7:10–16, 39. In verses 10–11, Paul draws on Jesus's teaching as follows: "To the married I give this charge (not I, but the Lord): the wife should not separate from her husband (but if she does, she should remain unmarried or else be reconciled to her husband), and the husband should not divorce his wife." As do Mark and Luke, Paul casts his statement in absolute terms, which makes Matthew the only New Testament document to include the "exception clause" regarding divorce for *porneia*. Husbands or wives should not divorce their spouses, the apostle writes, yet if they do, they must not remarry.

While 1 Corinthians 7:10–11 reads well under the assumption of a "no divorce, no remarriage" view, 1 Corinthians 7:12–16 complicates the discussion. There, Paul addresses the same issue in a slightly different context, that of a believer's desertion by an unbelieving spouse.[9] Since Jesus had not dealt with this specific question, Paul must adjudicate the situation himself ("I, not the Lord," 1 Cor. 7:12), which in no way diminishes the authoritative nature of Paul's apostolic pronouncement. According to Paul, a mixed marriage (i.e., one spouse is a believer while the other is not) is preferable to divorce (see 1 Pet. 3:1–2), because it provides a Christian environment for the children of this marital union (1 Cor. 7:14).[10] Yet if the unbelieving spouse insists on leaving, the believer is not to hold him or her back, because God's desire is for peace, and there is no guarantee that the unbeliever will eventually be saved (1 Cor. 7:15–16).[11]

Paul concludes, "But if the unbelieving partner separates, let it be so. In such cases the brother or sister is not enslaved [NIV: 'not bound']" (1 Cor. 7:15; the Greek word for *bound* is *douloō*). What is meant by "not bound" here? The parallel in 1 Corinthians 7:39 may help to shed some light on this question. There Paul writes, "A wife is *bound* [Gk. *deō*] to her husband as long as he lives. But if her husband dies, she is *free to be married* to whom she wishes, only in the Lord." The question at hand, then, is: Does Paul allow for marriage partners who have divorced on account of abandonment by an unbelieving spouse to remarry? As with the interpretation of the "exception clause" in Matthew 5:32; 19:9, interpreters differ in their answer to this question.

Competing Views

With regard to 1 Corinthians 7:15, a majority of evangelical scholars (i.e., those who hold to a "divorce and remarriage" view as described above) interpret the passage in conjunction with 1 Corinthians 7:39 as teaching that the innocent party is free to remarry. Advocates of this view contend that the Greek words *douloō* and *deō* are related and can be used interchangeably.[12] In accord with 1 Corinthians 7:39, then, abandonment, it is argued, results in a state in which the departing party is "dead" to the innocent spouse. In other words, according to this interpretation, abandonment by an unbelieving spouse dissolves the bonds of marriage and frees one to remarry another.

A minority of interpreters (i.e., those who hold to a "divorce, but no remarriage" or to a "no divorce, no remarriage" view as described above), however, assert that while in 1 Corinthians 7:15 Paul recognizes that acceptance of the gospel may result in abandonment by an unbelieving spouse (just as Jesus alluded to; see Luke 14:26–27; 18:29–30), he does not teach that this results in the dissolution of the bonds of marriage, nor does it yield the right to remarry. Advocates of this position note that Paul specifically prohibits remarriage in 1 Corinthians 7:10–11 and point out that when the apostle does explicitly refer to the possibility of remarriage in his writings, it is always in the context of the actual death of one of the marriage partners (Rom. 7:2; 1 Cor. 7:39). As such, while the abandoned party remains bound, there is no relational obligation to contest an unbelieving spouse's desire to depart.

Suggested Parameters

Recognizing that there is no "silver bullet" argument that will solve the debate over whether Paul allowed for remarriage after abandonment by an unbelieving spouse, we offer the following parameters for readers to consider in dealing with real-life situations and in the formation of their own views.

First, it should be noted that all orthodox views of 1 Corinthians 7:10–16, 39 acknowledge that in 1 Corinthians 7:15 Paul indicates that a divorce may occur if it is initiated by an unbelieving spouse. The debate related to this passage is not over whether such a divorce is permissible, but rather over that to which a believing party is bound—either to the marriage itself or to a relational obligation toward the departing spouse. Therefore, in 1 Corinthians 7:15 Paul is recognizing, much like Moses, that divorces do occur in a fallen world and is giving directions to govern such situations. When such a divorce does occur, then, the abandoned party ought not to be ostracized or looked down upon by the community of faith since the abandoned party did not seek a divorce but rather was the victim of abandonment.

Second, for those who do arrive at a view that allows for

remarriage after abandonment by an unbelieving spouse (which is the majority view of the modern church), such remarriages ought only to occur after prolonged attempts at reconciliation with the unbelieving spouse. After all, if reconciliation is explicitly held up by Paul as the ideal for believing spouses who divorce (1 Cor. 7:11), the standard for unbelieving spouses certainly should not be lower.

Third, those who honestly arrive at an interpretation of 1 Corinthians 7:15 that permits remarriage, and yet find reconciliation to the unbelieving spouse to be impossible, ought to feel free to remarry without guilt or censure by the church. Those with divergent interpretations of 1 Corinthians 7:15 should remember that those who do have freedom to remarry are not espousing a low view of marriage, nor are they acting contrary to the biblical text. Rather, they are acting in accord with their understanding of Scripture.

PRACTICAL IMPLICATIONS

After surveying the biblical materials on divorce and remarriage, we conclude that the creation narrative upholds, and Moses, Jesus, and Paul reaffirm, God's ordinance of marriage as a lifelong union between one man and one woman. Yet the debate over the morality of and/or reasons for divorce and remarriage in the modern church continues. We close this chapter with four principles that we trust will help those who are struggling with (or perhaps through) divorce and remarriage.

First, regardless of one's view of divorce and remarriage, we encourage all believers to bear in mind that while divorce and remarriage are life-altering events, even if one were to divorce and remarry sinfully, such action is not to be equated with the unpardonable sin. Therefore, while a sinful divorce and remarriage may result in lifelong consequences, the act itself is certainly pardonable upon confession of one's sin (1 John 1:9).

Second, while some Christians may be tempted to avoid the

entire discussion of divorce and remarriage—because of either the emotionally charged nature of the topic or the lack of scholarly consensus on the issue—we encourage all believers to carefully work through the biblical materials on divorce and remarriage.

Third, in such cases where divorce occurs as a result of a non-sexual sin (e.g., physical abuse), we encourage believers to remember that separation is not equivalent to divorce. In fact, in cases where one's life is being endangered by the actions of a sinning spouse, we conclude that separation is not only permissible but *morally required*. In such cases, we believe that it is the duty of the church to step in and minister to the sinned-against party in hopes of restoring the relationship or supporting the spouse in the event that the sinning party leaves.

Fourth, the question of divorce and remarriage is important also in the context of requirements for church leaders in the Pastoral Letters. Faithfulness in marriage, obedient children, and proper household management are regularly stressed in this regard (see esp. 1 Tim. 3:2–5; Titus 1:6). There is also a close link between the family and the church, which is God's "household" (1 Tim. 3:15), so that only those who are good husbands and fathers and who give adequate attention to managing their own homes are qualified to provide leadership for the church. While this would not automatically preclude a divorced, single, or childless married man from the pastorate, it does highlight the urgent need for one who holds the position of pastor to be truly a "one-woman type of man."[13]

GOD, MARRIAGE, FAMILY, AND THE CHURCH

How does God intend to relate marriage and family to the church? This is a question of theology (the doctrine of God) and ecclesiology (the doctrine of the church). A different but related question is this: How can churches today strengthen families? This question is one of method and application. In order to answer these two questions, it will be important to draw on the findings in previous chapters on the biblical theology of marriage and the family and to apply these findings to the biblical teaching on the nature of the church. It will also be important to address the practical questions regarding a biblical philosophy of church ministry and programs designed to strengthen marriages and families.

MARRIAGE, FAMILY, AND THE CHURCH

While some argue that the origins of the church reach back into Old Testament times, perhaps as far as Abraham, more properly the church should be seen to have its origin on the day of Pentecost subsequent to Jesus's ascension. In keeping with Old Testament prophecy, the Holy Spirit was poured out on the first nucleus of believers, accompanied by attesting signs and wonders (Acts 2).[1] This is supported, among other things, by the fact that Jesus uses the word "church" (*ekklēsia*) only twice in all the Gospels combined (Matt. 16:18; 18:17), there with the nontechnical sense "messianic community" and, at least in the first of these instances, in the future tense ("I will build my church"). Also, Luke never features the term *ekklēsia* in his Gospel, but uses it twenty-four times in Acts. This seems to suggest that he did not regard the church as present until the period covered in Acts.

Thus properly conceived, we find the bulk of the New Testament teaching regarding the church in Acts and the New Testament letters, particularly those written by the apostle Paul. One can then see that the existence of the church is predicated upon the saving, substitutionary death and resurrection of Jesus, in accordance with the Christian gospel (e.g., 1 Cor. 15:3–4). The New Testament is unequivocal that in order for anyone to become part of the church, he or she must be born again, that is, regenerated on the basis of his or her repentance and faith in the Lord Jesus Christ.[2] Any such person receives forgiveness of sins (Eph. 1:7), is justified (Rom. 5:1) and set apart for God's service (1 Cor. 1:2), and receives the Holy Spirit as well as spiritual gifts to use for the edification of the church (Eph. 1:13–14). Legitimate church membership, therefore, is predicated upon personal, individual repentance and faith in the Lord Jesus Christ, leading to regeneration and the indwelling of and gifting by the Holy Spirit (1 Cor. 12:4–13; Titus 3:4–7; see Rom. 8:9). When a person comes to faith, his or her familial state is of no consequence, whether married, single, divorced, or widowed.

What, then, is the church? In the New Testament, and particularly in Paul's teaching, we find several characterizations of the church and its nature and functions. Perhaps most prominent and pervasive is the Pauline teaching on the church as the "body of Christ" (e.g., Rom. 12:4–8; 1 Corinthians 12–14; Eph. 4:11–17; 5:30).[3] The emphasis in this description is on the relationship between Christ as the "head" and the church as his "body," indicating both Jesus's authority and lordship over the church and his provision for the church. Central in this provision is the Spirit's bestowal of particular spiritual gifts to every member of the body for the building up of the body to maturity (Eph. 4:13). Among the gifted members are those who serve the church as pastor-teachers (Eph. 4:11), whose role is to "equip his [God's] people for works of service" (Eph. 4:12 NIV). This metaphor thus stresses the church's unity with Christ and its submission to him as its head as well as the exercise of various spiritual gifts by its members. It is important to note that the work of equipping believers for the work of the ministry is said to be placed in the hands of spiritually gifted and duly appointed officers in the church. While fathers doubtless have a God-given responsibility to serve as spiritual leaders in their homes, the familial realm is distinct from the ecclesiastical realm where authority is vested in spiritually mature men who meet the qualifications for church leadership stipulated in passages such as 1 Timothy 3:1–7.

Another picture of the church found in the New Testament is that of the "household" or "family of God" (1 Tim. 3:4–5, 12, 14–15; 5:1–2; Titus 2:1–5). In 1 Timothy 3:15, Paul speaks of believers as "the household of God, which is the church of the living God, a pillar and buttress of the truth." He also establishes an important correlation between a man's oversight of his natural family and his qualification to oversee the affairs of the church in the role of elder (1 Tim. 3:4–5). In keeping with this "household" metaphor, Paul tells believers to relate to older people in the congregation as their "fathers" and "mothers" in Christ and to members of the same age or younger as "brothers" and "sisters" (1 Tim. 5:1–2). This harks back to Jesus's teaching that all those who do the will of the Father are his "brothers" and "sisters" (e.g., Mark 3:31–35; Luke 11:27–28).

Paul encourages older women to train young women as mothers would their daughters in the natural household, encouraging them to love their husbands and children, to be working at home, and to be submissive to their own husbands (Titus 2:3–5). The same is true for older men in the church in relation to younger men, who need to be grounded in the Word of God and learn to overcome the Evil One (e.g., 1 John 2:12–14). This picture accentuates more keenly the fact that the church is *built upon* the model of the natural household as its spiritual equivalent. This, as we will see, has important implications for the way in which God wants the church to function.

Beyond this, the New Testament uses a variety of other metaphors for the church, including that of a "new temple" (see 1 Pet. 2:4–5, 7) or the "temple of the Holy Spirit" (see 1 Cor. 3:16–17; Eph. 2:21–22) and that of the "bride of Christ" (see 2 Cor. 11:2; Eph. 5:32). In elaborating on the depiction of the church as the "new temple," Peter makes clear that the church is made up of those who "come to him" (1 Pet. 2:4) and "who believe" (v. 7). The church is thus made up of believing individuals; the passage makes no mention of families. The "bride of Christ" metaphor depicts the relationship between Christ and the church in terms of betrothal and consummation of a marriage at the end of time. One should not press the Scriptures to yield a theology of married couples being the primary building blocks of the church.

THE ROLES OF CHURCH AND FAMILY
The Role of the Church
In light of the survey of the biblical teaching on marriage and family in this book and of the brief survey of the nature of the church above, we return to the all-important question: What are the respective roles of the church and of the family, and how do the two relate to each other? We turn first to the church. The church is said in the New Testament to have a variety of roles.[4] First, it is called "the pillar and foundation of the truth" (1 Tim. 3:15 NIV). In a godless culture, it stands as a witness to God's revelation of truth and to God's redemption in Christ. Unlike the church, which is composed only of the regenerate, marriage, while divinely instituted in the beginning, is entered by regenerate and unregenerate alike. For this reason marriage and family as such cannot serve as sufficient vehicles of God's truth. It is the church, not the family,

that is therefore primarily charged with preaching the gospel to a lost world and fulfilling the Great Commission.

Second, the church is called to worship God and to evangelize and to disciple the nations (Matt. 28:16–20). The Eleven received this commission as representatives of the church, having (temporarily) left their natural family ties, which signified that following Jesus took absolute priority even over kinship relations. They received the Great Commission first and foremost as representatives of the nascent church, not as heads of families. Likewise, in Acts, Paul and Peter, Barnabas and Silas, and the other protagonists of the early church's mission are shown to engage in gospel preaching in their function as ministers of the gospel apart from their familial roles. In fact, several of them, including Paul and Timothy, were in all probability unmarried. Even in cases where those engaging in evangelistic preaching were married, marriage and family commitments were in some ways viewed not as the preferred vehicle or context but as a burden or necessary encumbrance in this life (see esp. 1 Cor. 7:32–35), and the roles of preacher/church planter and father/head of household were distinct. When Paul targeted entire households (Acts 10:24; 16:15, 31–34; 18:8), therefore, it was in all likelihood because he addressed himself primarily to the heads of household in his cultural surroundings in view of their influence on the other members of their household.

This continues to be a viable strategy today in many contexts, though it should be viewed primarily in terms of evangelistic method rather than as theologically normative or as the only biblical way to organize or evangelize. In terms of discipleship, too, it is the role of *the church* to disciple the nations (Matt. 28:19). Believing parents have an important role to play, but this does not alter the fact that it is the *church* that was given the charge to disciple individuals and to teach them to obey all that the Lord Jesus Christ commanded them to do (Matt. 28:20).

Third, the church is called to administer the ordinances of baptism and the Lord's Supper (e.g., Matt. 28:19; Luke 22:19;

Acts 2:42). This authority, likewise, is vested in the church. There is no indication in Scripture that fathers in their roles as heads of households are called upon to administer baptism or the Lord's Supper for their respective families. This is a function of the church and its leaders, not of individual or collective family units.

The Role of the Family

Now that we have identified the role of the church, let us turn briefly to the second question: What is the role of the family? The family and the church are not identical, nor does the family serve as the core structure of the church. What is the family's role in God's larger, overarching plan? In short, the family's primary role is *to care for the physical, social, and spiritual well-being of its members.* This includes the kind of provision, protection, and care with which the familial head was charged in Old Testament times and which is still characteristic of New Testament families (see Eph. 5:25–30).

The family is also the *environment for procreation and childrearing.* This, of course, is one of its core characteristics, to help fulfill God's creation mandate to humanity to "be fruitful and multiply and fill the earth and subdue it" (Gen. 1:28). This understanding is also supported by the fact that the curse following the fall affected both areas of male provision and female childbearing (Gen. 3:16– 19). While some, both in ancient times and today, have sought to disparage natural procreative functions and called those who would truly be spiritual to forsake their natural calling as wives and mothers (see, e.g., 1 Cor. 7:1, 12; 1 Tim. 2:15; 4:1, 3–4), God's Word holds the roles of father and mother in high esteem. The church will therefore uphold God's noble vision of marriage and the family in stark contrast to much of the surrounding world, which finds greater significance in the pursuit of self-fulfillment, material wealth, or other substitutes for God's true calling.

Finally, anyone in a given family who is spiritually converted is to *use his or her influence in his natural family to witness to Christ and to lead other family members to him* (1 Cor. 7:14; 1 Pet. 3:1–6). Thus, families find a place in the Christian reality as the redeemed exercise influence in the familial sphere.

The family is indeed of vital importance for the survival and flourishing of human society, and families that pattern themselves after God's revealed will in his Word are absolutely critical for sustaining a vibrant church and a morally intact society. At the same time, there should be no confusion as to what the family is and is not: *The family of God is not a family of nuclear families but a gathering or body of true regenerate believers organized in a given locale as a local congregation under duly constituted leadership regardless of their family status.* The family and the church each have distinct roles and serve distinct purposes in God's plan. They each have particular spheres of operation and powers and authorities. While there is a certain amount of overlap, these two entities should therefore not be confused or unduly collapsed into one.

THE CHURCH AND FAMILY MINISTRY

Having adjudicated the respective roles and proper relationship between the church and the family, follow-up questions naturally arise: How, then, can the church support the family? And how can the family undergird the church? It goes without saying that due to the vital importance of marriage and family in God's plan from the beginning, the church should do everything it can to strengthen the marriage bond and family ties. It should teach young couples the proper biblical roles of husband and wife and God's plan for them to establish a family and should encourage existing marriages and families to witness to God's goodness, wisdom, and faithfulness in Christ to the surrounding culture. It should pattern itself after God's plan for the natural household in which, as mentioned, the older, mature generation trains and disciples the younger members. It should also recognize that some of its members may be called to remain unmarried for the sake of God's kingdom and integrate them fully in the life of the church.

It is also evident that the church in the West has often not done a very good job of nurturing marriages and natural family units. It has frequently failed to affirm the husband's headship in the home and the father's central role in the family. As such, the unbelieving world—which has witnessed the disintegration of God's established order in the home and the demise of male leadership in the family—and the church—with its failure to affirm, nurture, and encourage biblical patterns for marriage and the family—have sadly joined forces to further weaken the biblical foundation for marriage and the family in our culture. Without collapsing the distinctions between the church and the home, the church ought to make every effort to make strengthening marriages and families a vital part of its mission. In particular, it should respect the need for families to spend adequate time together so the parents can nurture their children spiritually. Having a church calendar full of events and programs that leaves little time for the family and has its members running ragged will do little to strengthen the vital family bond.

What seems beyond dispute, then, is that the world is weakening marriages and families in many ways, and that the church often fails to counteract these disintegrative forces by neglecting to conceive of its mission in terms that strengthen marriages and families. (At the same time, it should be noted that some churches are well aware of this need and are making a sincere effort to encourage families.) What is less, clear, however, is *how* the church can reverse this trend. In this regard, it will be important to distinguish between theology and method. With regard to *theology*, it will be important to be grounded in the biblical teaching on the nature and function of the church. With regard to *method*, there should be a certain amount of flexibility and openness to a variety of approaches. It will also be important not to confuse theology with method and not to charge those who differ from us in method with being unbiblical simply because they do not agree on the specific remedy.

What is needed is a church model that strengthens and supports marriages and families and does so on the basis of a robust biblical understanding of the nature of the church. The man's leadership in marriage and the home and the need for wives to submit to their husbands and for children to obey their parents are part of this. The importance of intergenerational or multigenerational ministry that does not unnecessarily segment the church into disjunctive, isolated individual units but builds on natural affinity groups, including flesh-and-blood ties, is vital as well. At the same time, the local church leadership has the right and the authority to devise ways to disciple its members, including young people, which may legitimately involve gathering them together and instructing them in peer group settings.

PRACTICAL IMPLICATIONS

We conclude with a few questions that all churches would do well to ask: (1) Do we acknowledge singleness as a valid spiritual gift and singles as church members and citizens of the kingdom on par with families, or do we privilege families and treat singles as somehow deficient and second-class? (2) Do we reach out to everyone regardless of their stage of life, race, and class, or only to certain people in keeping with the demographic makeup of the majority of church members, be it those of a certain socioeconomic profile, or schooling choice, or any other grouping? In other words, is our church *genuinely inclusive* in keeping with Jesus's proclamation of the kingdom of God? (3) Do we understand and practice Jesus's teaching about the kingdom and the New Testament teaching about the church? Or is our model predominantly or exclusively predicated upon Old Testament models?

CONCLUSION

Uniting All Things in Him

SUMMARY

We have come to the end of our discussion of marriage and the family. As we noted at the outset, for the first time in its history Western civilization is confronted with the need to define the meaning of the terms *marriage* and *family*. The cultural crisis that rages concerning the definitions of these terms is symptomatic of an underlying spiritual crisis that gnaws at the foundations of our once-shared societal values. In this spiritual cosmic conflict, Satan and his minions actively oppose the Creator's design for marriage and the family and seek to distort God's image as it is reflected in God-honoring Christian marriages and families. In light of the current confusion over marriage and the family, there is a need for the kind of biblical and integrative treatment the present volume attempts to provide.

Human sexuality and relationships are rooted in the eternal will of the Creator as expressed in the way in which God made men and women. The biblical concept of marriage is a sacred bond between a man and a woman, instituted by and publicly entered into before God (whether or not this is acknowledged by the married couple), normally consummated by sexual intercourse. Rather than being merely a contract that is made for a limited period of time, marriage is a sacred bond that is characterized by permanence, sacredness, intimacy, mutuality, and exclusiveness.

Scripture plainly reveals that the bearing and raising of children are elemental parts of God's plan for marriage. The Old Testament presents children as a blessing from the Lord, and the responsibilities of fathers, mothers, and children are spelled out in some detail. In the New Testament, parents are urged to bring up their children in the nurture and admonition of the Lord (Eph. 6:4), and women are to place special priority on their God-given calling as mothers and homemakers (1 Tim. 2:15; Titus 2:4–5). Both Testaments remind fathers of their sacred duty to provide for their children as well as to enforce discipline (Prov. 13:24; 2 Cor. 12:14; Heb. 12:6).

In the area of reproduction, Scripture is clear that life begins at conception and that abortion is morally unacceptable. While contraception in general is a legitimate Christian option, this does not mean that every form of birth control is morally acceptable for believers. Only those devices that are contraceptive rather than abortive in nature are legitimate Christian options. Artificial reproductive technologies likewise raise a variety of complex ethical issues and call for careful adjudication in order to determine which are and are not ethically permissible for believers today. The Bible presents adoption as an honored avenue for glorifying God and building a Christian family, especially for couples having difficulty conceiving children of their own.

With regard to Christian parenting, we stressed the importance of cultivating a relationship with our children and of relying on the Spirit's guidance in parenting. In our treatment of single parenting, we adduced biblical teaching on God's concern for the fatherless and discussed some of the ways in which the church can assist single parents. We also discussed the topic of spiritual warfare pertaining to marriage and the family. Since marriage is such an important component of God's economy, the Devil continually attacks this divinely instituted human relationship. Therefore, believers need to be ready to defend their marriages as well as the larger institution of matrimony.

We also discussed singleness as it pertains to those who are not yet married, those who are widowed, or those who remain permanently unmarried (whether by choice or circumstance). While a couple is to refrain from sexual relations prior to entering into marriage, and while widowed individuals are permitted—in certain cases even encouraged—to remarry, permanent singleness (celibacy) is considered by both Jesus and Paul to be a special gift from God, though not a necessary requirement for church office (see 1 Tim. 3:2, 12; Titus 1:6). By promoting undistracted devotion to the Lord, singleness can actually be a unique opportunity for kingdom service (1 Cor. 7:32–35).

Creation teaches that heterosexuality, rather than homosexuality, is God's pattern for men and women. The sexes are created in distinctness, which must not be blurred or obliterated, and humanity exists as male and female for the purpose of complementarity and procreation, neither of which can be properly realized in same-sex sexual relationships. Moreover, the divine image is imprinted on man *as male and female*, so that homosexual unions fall short of reflecting God's own likeness as unity in diversity.

Because marriage is a divinely ordained covenant institution (Gen. 1:28; 2:24) rather than merely a human contractual agreement, divorce is permissible only in certain carefully delineated exceptional cases (if at all). Possible legitimate reasons for divorce include sexual marital unfaithfulness (adultery) as well as desertion by an unbeliever. Even in those cases, however, reconciliation is to be the aim, and divorce is only permitted, not commanded. In all cases, divorce *remains the least preferable option*, for it falls short of God's design for marriage and the family. Where divorce is biblically legitimate, however, most would agree that so is remarriage. The latter is apropos also in case of spousal death, "only in the Lord" (1 Cor. 7:39 NASB).

The final chapter dealt with the respective roles of the church and the family and briefly addressed the question of how those in church leadership can support and strengthen marriages and families.

Both Testaments in Scripture present a coherent body of teachings pertaining to marriage and the family. From the garden of Eden, to Israel, to Jesus, to the early church, to Paul, all uphold a very high standard in this crucial area of life. While countless times individuals did and will fall short of God's ideal, Scripture makes clear that the Creator's standard for marriage and family remains intact—it was instituted at creation and is expected of humankind today. In this as well as in other areas, in the first century as today, Christianity towers above pagan cultures and displays the character of a holy God in the lives and relationships of his people.

CONCLUSION

We have come a long way in our understanding of the biblical teaching on marriage and the family. We can do no better than conclude by praying for our families Paul's prayer for the Ephesian believers, who were also the recipients of the apostle's marvelous instructions regarding marriage, childrearing, and spiritual warfare:

> For this reason I bow my knees before the Father, *from whom every family in heaven and on earth is named*, that according to the riches of his glory he may grant you to be strengthened with power through his Spirit in your inner being, so that Christ may dwell in your hearts through faith—that you, being rooted and grounded in love, may have strength to comprehend with all the saints what is the breadth and length and height and depth, and to know the love of Christ that surpasses knowledge, that you may be filled with all the fullness of God.
>
> Now to him who is able to do far more abundantly than all that we ask or think, according to the power at work within us, *to him be glory* in the church and in Christ Jesus *throughout all generations*, forever and ever. Amen. (Eph. 3:14–21)

NOTES

Thanks are due Jake Pratt for his help with abridging this volume. For an extensive list of resources for further study, see the second edition of Andreas J. Köstenberger with David W. Jones, *God, Marriage, and Family: Rebuilding the Biblical Foundation* (Wheaton, IL: Crossway, 2010), 289–311.

Chapter 1: Marriage in the Bible

1. See Matt. 19:5–6; Mark 10:9; 1 Cor. 6:16; Eph. 5:31; see Mal. 2:10–16, esp. v. 10.
2. See Raymond C. Ortlund Jr., "Male-Female Equality and Male Headship," in John Piper and Wayne Grudem, eds., *Recovering Biblical Manhood and Womanhood* (Wheaton, IL: Crossway, 1991), 95–112.
3. See Millard J. Erickson, *Christian Theology*, 2d ed. (Grand Rapids: Baker, 1998), 532–34; see also his survey of the three major views on the image of God in man, 520–29.
4. See Anthony Hoekema, *Created in God's Image* (Grand Rapids: Eerdmans, 1986), 73.
5. See James B. Hurley, *Man and Woman in Biblical Perspective* (Grand Rapids: Zondervan, 1981), 210–12.
6. See chapter 12, "One Man and One Woman," in Christopher Ash, *Marriage: Sex in the Service of God* (Leicester: Inter-Varsity, 2003).
7. See Ash, *Marriage*, 348–55, who rightly observes that the "one flesh" union between husband and wife denotes both the entering into a public family bond and consummation by sexual intercourse.
8. See Andreas J. Köstenberger, "Ascertaining Women's God-Ordained Roles: An Interpretation of 1 Timothy 2:15," *Bulletin of Biblical Research* 7 (1997): 107–44.
9. See Susan T. Foh, "What Is the Woman's Desire (Gen 3:16, 4:7)?" *Westminster Theological Journal* 37 (1975): 376–83.
10. See Daniel I. Block, "Marriage and Family in Ancient Israel," in Ken M. Campbell, ed., *Marriage and Family in the Biblical World* (Downers Grove, IL: InterVarsity, 2003), 40–48. Also see the discussion in chap. 3 below.
11. See, e.g., Gen. 16:1, 16; 17:17, 19, 21; 21:2–3, 5, 7, 9; 22:20, 23; 24:15, 24, 47; 25:2, 12.

12. For a brief survey see Charles H. H. Scobie, *The Ways of Our God* (Grand Rapids: Eerdmans, 2003), 807, who states that the ideal of monogamy is established in Gen. 2:24, assumed in the Law (Deut. 28:54, 56) and in the Prophets (Jer. 5:8; 6:11; Mal. 2:14), and upheld in the Wisdom Literature (Prov. 5:18; 31:10–31; Eccles. 9:9).
13. See also Jesus's citation and interpretation of Gen. 2:24 in Matt. 19:4–6 (see also Mark 10:6–9).
14. For a discussion of adultery in the Old Testament see Ash, *Marriage*, 356–64.
15. The apostle Peter sums up the Old Testament pattern as follows: "For this is how the holy women who hoped in God used to adorn themselves, by submitting to their own husbands, as Sarah obeyed Abraham, calling him lord" (1 Pet. 3:5–6).
16. The book of Proverbs, too, includes a section extolling sex within the framework of a faithful, committed marriage relationship and warning against adultery (Prov. 5:15–20).
17. See especially Foh, "What Is the Woman's Desire?" See also Ash, *Marriage*, 277–79, esp. his discussion of the three ways of understanding the phrase "he shall rule over you" on 278.
18. This in no way amounts to a license for husbands to abuse their wives physically or in any other way, nor does it preclude the necessity for wives to separate from their abusive husbands in order to avoid serious harm.
19. Note that Gentiles comprise the majority of Paul's readership in Ephesians.
20. See Andreas J. Köstenberger, "What Does It Mean to Be Filled with the Spirit? A Biblical Investigation," *Journal for the Evangelical Theological Society* 40 (1997): 229–40 for a detailed discussion of Eph. 5:18 and related passages.
21. See esp. the definitive, virtually unanswerable refutation of the notion of "mutual submission" by spouses in Ash, *Marriage*, 307–10.
22. In that context, husbands' love is further defined as not being harsh with one's wife (see 1 Pet. 3:7).
23. See esp. Ortlund, "Male-Female Equality and Male Headship," 95–112, esp. 106–11.
24. For a detailed discussion, see Andreas J. Köstenberger, "The Mystery of Christ and the Church: Head and Body, 'One Flesh,'" *TrinJ* NS (1991): 79–94.

Chapter 2: Marriage and Sex

1. Augustine, "On the Good of Marriage," in *The Nicene and Post-Nicene Fathers*, ed. Philip Schaff (Grand Rapids: Eerdmans, repr. 1980 [1887]), First Series, vol. 3, 397–413. Attitudes to sexuality, marriage, and family in the patristic period are chronicled by Peter Brown, *The Body and Society* (London: Faber & Faber, 1990).

2. See the "Doctrine on the Sacrament of Matrimony" from the twenty-fourth session of the Council of Trent in James Waterworth, ed. and trans., *The Canons and Decrees of the Sacred and Oecumenical Council of Trent* (London: Dolman, 1848), 192–232. For a basic presentation of Roman Catholic sacramental theology see Alan Schreck, *Basics of the Faith: A Catholic Catechism* (Ann Arbor, MI: Servant, 1987), 147–82.

3. Schreck, *Basics of the Faith*, 152.

4. See Germain Grisez, "The Christian Family as Fulfillment of Sacramental Marriage," *Studies in Christian Ethics* 9, no. 1 (1996): 23–33.

5. See Andreas J. Köstenberger, "The Mystery of Christ and the Church: Head and Body, 'One Flesh,'" *TrinJ* NS (1991): 87.

6. See John Witte Jr., *From Sacrament to Contract: Marriage, Religion, and Law in the Western Tradition* (Louisville: Westminster John Knox, 1997), who argues that Western Christianity has moved steadily from a sacramental to a contractual view of marriage; Paul F. Palmer, "Christian Marriage: Contract or Covenant?" *Theological Studies* 33, no. 4 (Dec. 1972): 617–65; Laura S. Levitt, "Covenant or Contract? Marriage as Theology," *Cross Currents* 48, no. 2 (Summer 1998): 169–84.

7. See David Instone-Brewer, *Divorce and Remarriage in the Bible* (Grand Rapids: Eerdmans, 2002), 1–19.

8. See Gary D. Chapman, *Covenant Marriage* (Nashville: Broadman, 2003), 8–10; see also the more popular treatment in Fred Lowery, *Covenant Marriage* (West Monroe, LA: Howard, 2002), 81–95.

9. Gordon R. Dunstan, "Marriage Covenant," *Theology* 78 (May 1975): 244.

10. See Gordon P. Hugenberger, *Marriage as a Covenant* (Grand Rapids: Baker, 1998 [1994]). See also David Atkinson, *To Have and to Hold* (Grand Rapids: Eerdmans, 1979); and John MacArthur Jr., *Matthew 16–23*, The MacArthur New Testament Commentary (Chicago: Moody, 1988), 167.

11. See esp. chap. 15 in Ash, *Marriage*. For a list of covenantal traits of marriage see David P. Gushee, *Getting Marriage Right* (Grand Rapids: Baker, 2004), 136–38.

12. John R. W. Stott, "Marriage and Divorce," in *Involvement*, vol. 2 (Old Tappan, NJ: Revell, 1984), 163.

13. Paul R. Williamson, "Covenant," *New Dictionary of Biblical Theology*,

ed. T. Desmond Alexander and Brian S. Rosner (Leicester; Downers Grove, IL: InterVarsity, 2000), 420.

14. Instone-Brewer, *Divorce and Remarriage in the Bible*, 17.
15. E.g., Jer. 31:32; Ezek. 16:8, 59–62; Hos. 2:18–22; Eph. 5:22–33; see 1 Sam. 18–20. See esp. Hugenberger, *Marriage as a Covenant*, 294–312. On Ezekiel 16, see Marvin H. Pope, "Mixed Marriage Metaphor in Ezekiel 16," *Fortunate the Eyes That See*, ed. Astrid Beck (Grand Rapids: Eerdmans, 1995), 384–99.
16. See Hugenberger, *Marriage as a Covenant*, 216–79.
17. See Michael V. Fox, *Proverbs 1–9*, Anchor Bible (New York: Doubleday, 2000), 120–21; and the very thorough discussion in Hugenberger, *Marriage as a Covenant*, 296–302.
18. Fox, *Proverbs 1–9*, 121. Hence, in its biblical context, the notion of covenant includes that of a contractual arrangement. See also Pieter A. Verhoef, *The Books of Haggai and Malachi*, New International Commentary on the Old Testament (Grand Rapids: Eerdmans, 1987), 274, who notes that marriage qualifies as "a covenant of God" in that it is contracted in submission to the revealed will of God (Ex. 20:14) and with the expectation of his blessing (Gen. 1:28); Hugenberger, *Marriage as a Covenant*, esp. 27–47; and Daniel I. Block, "Marriage and Family in Ancient Israel," in Ken M. Campbell, ed., *Marriage and Family in the Biblical World* (Downers Grove, IL: InterVarsity, 2003), 44, who states unequivocally that "ancient Israelites viewed marriage as a covenant relationship," citing Prov. 2:17 and Mal. 2:14.
19. For a good book on the "what" of sex, see Linda Dillow and Lorraine Pintus, *Intimate Issues* (Colorado Springs, CO: WaterBrook, 1999).
20. Ash, *Marriage*, 103–4.
21. Geoffrey W. Bromiley, *God and Marriage* (Grand Rapids: Eerdmans, 1980), *xiii.*
22. Ash, *Marriage*.
23. Ibid.
24. See Andreas J. Köstenberger, "On the Alleged Apostolic Origins of Celibacy," in *Studies in John and Gender*, Studies in Biblical Literature 38 (New York: Peter Lang, 2001), 173–83. For negative attitudes toward sex, see, e.g., Augustine, "On the Good of Marriage" sect. 5, 6, 8, 23, 25.
25. See Peter Brown, *Body and Society*; D. S. Bailey, *The Man-Woman Relation in Christian Thought* (London: Longmans, Green, 1959).
26. For a discussion of the relationship between the procreational and relational aspects of marriage see Ash, *Marriage*, 200–204. The notion

of a husband's glad, grateful enjoyment of his wife as God's gift is firmly entrenched in biblical wisdom: see, e.g., Prov. 5:15–19; Eccl. 9:9; and the Song of Solomon.

27. Ash, *Marriage*, 110–11, adduces Prov. 6:20–35; 1 Cor. 7:2; and 1 Thess. 4:6.

28. Ibid., 206–7.

29. Ibid., 212–14.

30. Dillow and Pintus, *Intimate Issues*, 199–204. See also Dennis P. Hollinger, *Meaning of Sex* (Grand Rapids: Baker, 2009), 155–61.

Chapter 3: Family in the Bible

1. This rules out cohabiting couples as well as same-sex marriages or domestic partnerships. See George Rekers, *The Christian World View of the Family* (Sunnyvale, CA: The Coalition on Revival, 1989), 6: "We affirm that the Biblical definition of family is the nuclear family of a heterosexual married couple with its natural and adopted children, together with family branches consisting of all nuclear families descended from common ancestors," http://65.175.91.69/ Reformation_net/COR_Docs/Christian_Worldview_Family.pdf.

2. Of course, spiritually speaking, all believers have been adopted into God's family and are brothers and sisters in Christ.

3. See Daniel I. Block, "Marriage and Family in Ancient Israel," in Ken M. Campbell, ed., *Marriage and Family in the Biblical World* (Downers Grove, IL: InterVarsity, 2003), 35. The following discussion is indebted to this work.

4. Ibid., 41.

5. Ibid., 47.

6. Ibid., 53–55.

7. Ibid., 66–68.

8. See ibid., 77–78.

9. See ibid., 80–82.

10. Ibid., 93.

11. For a lucid discussion of the teaching of the book of Proverbs with a view of training young men in wisdom, see ibid., 89–92.

12. The Scripture references in parentheses are illustrative rather than exhaustive. The attributes are listed in order of first occurrence in the book of Proverbs.

13. See especially the helpful study "Parent and Children" in Derek Kidner, *Proverbs*, Tyndale Old Testament Commentary (Leicester; Downers Grove, IL: InterVarsity, 1964), 50–52.

14. On gender roles in Palestinian and geographically related Jewish

traditions, see Craig S. Keener, "Marriage," in Craig A. Evans and Stanley E. Porter, eds., *Dictionary of New Testament Background* (Downers Grove, IL: InterVarsity, 2000), 690.

15. Luke 14:26; see Matt. 10:37: "*loves* father or mother . . . son or daughter *more* than me."

16. See Stephen C. Barton, "Family," *Dictionary of Jesus and the Gospels*, ed. Joel B. Green, Scot McKnight, and I. Howard Marshall (Downers Grove: InterVarsity, 1992), 226–29.

17. Examples include Jairus's daughter in Mark 5:21–24, 35–43; the daughter of a Syrophoenician woman in Mark 7:24–30; and a demon-possessed boy in Mark 9:14–29.

18. See James Francis, "Children and Childhood in the New Testament," in *The Family in Theological Perspective*, ed. Stephen C. Barton (Edinburgh: T & T Clark, 1996), 75, who correlates this to the recollection of Israel's own experience with God in passages such as Deut. 7:7–8; Hos. 11:1–4; Ezek. 16:3–8; and Ps. 74:1.

19. This does not mean, of course, that rendering Christianity respectable in the surrounding culture is the *supreme* or *only* principle at stake in living out one's marriage relationship according to biblical truth and revelation. Even if certain aspects of the Christian message or Christian living are countercultural, this may challenge the surrounding culture to ponder the distinctness and difference of the gospel.

20. See Peter T. O'Brien, *The Letter to the Ephesians*, Pillar New Testament Commentary (Grand Rapids: Eerdmans, 1999), 439.

21. Ibid., 441.

22. Ibid., 440–41.

23. Ibid., 440.

24. Andrew T. Lincoln, *Ephesians*, Word Biblical Commentary (Dallas, TX: Word, 1990), 406.

25. See Andreas J. Köstenberger, "Ascertaining Women's God-Ordained Roles: An Interpretation of 1 Timothy 2:15," *Bulletin of Biblical Research* 7 (1997): 142–44, esp. 143.

26. Ibid.

27. Ibid., 143.

28. See 2 Pet. 2:19; Rom. 6:18, 22; 1 Cor. 7:15; Gal. 4:3. This attribute is also required of elders and deacons (1 Tim. 3:3, 8).

Chapter 4: Reproduction and Parenting

1. James K. Hoffmeier, ed., *Abortion* (Grand Rapids: Baker, 1987), 55, cited in Charles H. H. Scobie, *The Ways of Our God* (Grand Rapids: Eerdmans, 2003), 801.

2. Scobie, *Ways of Our God*, 801.

3. C. Hassell Bullock, "Abortion and Old Testament Prophetic and Poetic Literature," in Hoffmeier, ed., *Abortion*, 68.

4. See Andreas Lindemann, "'Do Not Let a Woman Destroy the Unborn Babe in Her Belly': Abortion in Ancient Judaism and Christianity," *Studia theologica* 49 (1995): 253–71.

5. Pope Paul VI, *Humanae Vitae* 14–17.

6. R. Albert Mohler Jr., "Can Christians Use Birth Control? (Parts 1 and 2)," March 29 and 30, 2004, http://www.albertmohler.com/radio_ archive.html.

7. For a sensitive treatment of involuntary childlessness see Christopher Ash, *Marriage: Sex in the Service of God* (Leicester: Inter-Varsity, 2003), 180–81.

8. This is hardly satisfactory, however, since, to be consistent, the proponents of this kind of argument would also have to conclude that the use of any medical intervention for a medical problem is likewise inappropriate.

9. Karen Dawson, *Reproductive Technology: The Science, the Ethics, the Law and the Social Issues* (Melbourne: VCTA Publishing, Macmillan Education Australia, 1995), 49.

10. Scott B. Rae, *Moral Choices: An Introduction to Ethics*, 2d ed. (Grand Rapids: Zondervan, 2000), 154.

11. See esp. Russell D. Moore, *Adopted for Life: The Priority of Adoption for Christian Families and Churches* (Wheaton, IL: Crossway, 2009).

12. See John 1:12–13; Rom. 8:14–17, 29; Gal. 3:23–36; 4:1–7; Eph. 1:5; 1 John 3:1–2, 10; 5:19.

13. 1 Corinthians 12–14; Romans 12; Ephesians 4.

14. See F. Charles Fensham, "Widow, Orphan, and the Poor in Ancient Near Eastern Legal and Wisdom Literature," *Journal of Near Eastern Studies* 21 (1962): 129–39; Harold V. Bennett, *Injustice Made Legal* (Grand Rapids: Eerdmans, 2002).

15. See Susan Graham Mathis, "Good Samaritans for Single Parents," *Focus on the Family*, April 2004, 20–21. *Focus on the Family* magazine has a special edition just for single parents, which can be ordered at http://www.family.org.

16. For information about the benefits of spanking from a Christian perspective see Walter L. Larimore, "Is Spanking Actually Harmful to Children?" *Focus on the Family*, 2002.

17. Paul D. Wegner, "Discipline in the Book of Proverbs: 'To Spank or

Not to Spank,'" *Journal of the Evangelical Theological Society* 48, no. 4 (December 2005): 715–32.

18. On same-sex marriage, see, e.g., Glenn T. Stanton and Bill Maier, *Marriage on Trial* (Downers Grove, IL: InterVarsity, 2004) and James R. White and Jeffrey D. Niell, *The Same-Sex Controversy* (Minneapolis: Bethany, 2002).

Chapter 5: Singleness

1. Rose M. Kreider and Tavia Simmons, *Marital Status: 2000* (Washington DC: U.S. Census Bureau, 1993), 3.
2. Daniel I. Block, "Marriage and Family in Ancient Israel," in Ken M. Campbell, ed., *Marriage and Family in the Biblical World* (Downers Grove, IL: InterVarsity, 2003), 57n113.
3. Block (ibid., 71) notes that almost one-third of the occurrences of the word for *widow*, *'almānâ*, are found in Mosaic legislation providing for the well-being of other vulnerable groups, such as orphans, aliens, and Levites.
4. See ibid., 93–94; David W. Chapman, "Marriage and Family in Second Temple Judaism," in Ken M. Campbell, ed., *Marriage and Family in the Biblical World* (Downers Grove, IL: InterVarsity, 2003), 216–17.
5. See Ex. 22:22; Deut. 14:29; 16:11, 14; 24:19–21; 27:19; Isa. 1:17; Jer. 22:3; Zech. 7:10.
6. See Ex. 22:23; Pss. 68:5; 146:9; Prov. 15:25; Mal. 3:5.
7. S. Safrai, "Home and Family," *The Jewish People of the First Century*, ed. S. Safrai and M. Stern (Philadelphia: Fortress, 1987), 748. See *m. Ketub.* 13:5; *b. Ketub.* 82b.
8. See Block, "Marriage and Family in Ancient Israel," 49–52.
9. Thus, Paul can stipulate that church leaders are to be faithful husbands (1 Tim 3:2, 12).
10. See Barry Danylak, *Redeeming Singleness* (Wheaton, IL: Crossway, 2010), chap. 6.
11. Barry Danylak, *A Biblical Theology of Singleness*, Grove Series B 45 (Cambridge, UK: Grove, 2007), 8–12.
12. Ibid., 14.
13. Ibid., 16.
14. Ibid., 17.
15. Ibid., 24–25.
16. Ibid., 26.
17. Ibid., 27.
18. Dennis and Barbara Rainey, in *Passport2Purity* (Little Rock, AR: FamilyLife, 2004), an excellent resource that comes highly

recommended, make a strong case that sexual purity prior to marriage does not merely entail refraining from sexual intercourse but abstaining from sexual activity altogether.

19. For specific steps in dealing with sexual temptation, see the 2d ed. of *God, Marriage, and Family* (Wheaton, IL: Crossway, 2010), 189–90.
20. This is borne out amply by Old Testament teaching regarding widows (Ex. 22:22–23; Deut. 10:8; 14:29; 24:17–21; 26:12, 13; 27:19; etc.).
21. This, of course, does not affect our comments in the chapter on biblically legitimate or illegitimate divorce and the scriptural teaching on remarriage. Specifically, single parents who are the guilty party in a divorce should not be encouraged to remarry but to be reconciled to their former spouse.
22. See David P. Gushee, *Getting Marriage Right: Realistic Counsel for Saving and Strengthening Relationships* (Grand Rapids: Baker, 2004), 57–83.
23. See also John F. MacArthur, *Different by Design* (Colorado Springs: Chariot Victor, 1994), 98–106.

Chapter 6: Homosexuality

1. For a helpful treatment, see Dennis P. Hollinger, *The Meaning of Sex* (Grand Rapids: Baker, 2009), chap. 7.
2. Gen. 9:20–27; 19:4–11; Lev. 18:22; 20:13; Deut. 23:17–18; Judg. 19:22–25; 1 Kings 14:24; 15:12; 22:46; 2 Kings 23:7; Job 36:14; Ezek. 16:50 (perhaps also Ezek. 18:12; 33:26); Rom. 1:26–27; 1 Cor. 6:9–10; 1 Tim. 1:9–10; 2 Pet. 2:6; Jude 7; Rev. 21:8; 22:15. See Robert A. J. Gagnon, *The Bible and Homosexual Practice* (Nashville: Abingdon, 2001), 432.
3. See Isa. 1:9–10; 3:9; 13:19; Jer. 23:14; 49:18; 50:40; Lam. 4:6; Ezek. 16:46, 48–49, 53, 55–56; Amos 4:11; Zeph. 2:9; Matt. 10:15; 11:23–24; Luke 10:12; 17:29; Rom. 9:29 (quoting Isa. 1:9); 2 Pet. 2:6; Jude 7; Rev. 11:8.
4. Walter Barnett, *Homosexuality and the Bible* (Wallingford, PA: Pendle Hill, 1979), 8–9.
5. D. Sherwin Bailey, *Homosexuality and the Western Christian Tradition* (London: Longmans, Green, 1955), 4.
6. We have no record of Jesus's commenting on the subject, which suggests that this was not a controversial issue in first-century Palestinian Judaism (though see chap. 3, "The Witness of Jesus," in Gagnon, *Bible and Homosexual Practice*, 191.
7. See Everett Ferguson, *Backgrounds of Early Christianity*, 2d ed. (Grand Rapids: Eerdmans, 1993), 63–74.
8. Some of the subsequent analysis is indebted to Gordon D. Fee, *The First Letter to the Corinthians*, New International Commentary on the New Testament (Grand Rapids: Eerdmans, 1987), 242–45.

9. John Boswell, *Christianity, Social Tolerance, and Homosexuality* (Chicago: University of Chicago Press, 1980), 140–41.

10. Robin Scroggs, *The New Testament and Homosexuality* (Philadelphia: Fortress, 1983), 106–8; see also Graydon F. Snyder, *First Corinthians* (Atlanta: Mercer University Press, 1992), 72–73.

11. See Bailey, *Homosexuality and the Western Christian Tradition*.

12. John J. McNeill, *The Church and the Homosexual* (Kansas City, MO: Sheed, Andrews and McMeel, 1976), 53–56. See also Dale B. Martin, *"Arsenokoitēs* and *Malakos*: Meaning and Consequences," *Biblical Ethics and Homosexuality: Listening to Scripture*, ed. Robert L. Brawley (Louisville, KY: Westminster, 1996), 129–30.

13. William L. Petersen, "Can ᾿Αρσενοκοίται Be Translated by 'Homosexuals'?" *Vigiliae Christianae* 40 (1986): 187–91 (quote from p. 189).

14. For helpful materials, see Joe Dallas, *Desires in Conflict* (Eugene, OR: Harvest, 2003); Anne Paulk, *Restoring Sexual Identity* (Eugene, OR: Harvest, 2003); and Anita Worthen and Bob Davies, *Someone I Love Is Gay* (Downers Grove, IL: InterVarsity, 1996).

Chapter 7: Divorce and Remarriage

1. See Gordon J. Wenham, "Gospel Definitions of Adultery and Women's Rights," *Expository Times* 95 (1984): 330.

2. See John S. Feinberg and Paul D. Feinberg, *Ethics for a Brave New World* (Wheaton, IL: Crossway, 1993), 313.

3. E.g., Paul Ramsey, *Basic Christian Ethics* (Louisville, KY: Westminster, 1993 [1950]), 71.

4. William A. Heth, "Jesus on Divorce: How My Mind Has Changed," *Southern Baptist Journal of Theology* 6, no. 1 (Spring 2002): 16. See also Feinberg and Feinberg, *Ethics for a Brave New World*, 335–36 and the discussion below.

5. The qualifying phrase "for any cause" is missing from the parallel in Mark 10:2.

6. John W. Shepard, *The Christ of the Gospels* (Grand Rapids: Eerdmans, 1946 [1939]), 452; D. A. Carson, "Matthew," in *The Expositor's Bible Commentary*, rev. ed. (Grand Rapids: Zondervan, 2010), 466; William L. Lane, *The Gospel according to Mark*, New International Commentary on the New Testament 2 (Grand Rapids: Eerdmans, 1974), 354. Mark focuses more on the political dimension of the interchange, while Matthew emphasizes the rabbinic legal issue (see Robert H. Gundry, *Matthew: A Commentary on His Handbook for a Mixed Church under*

Persecution (Grand Rapids: Eerdmans, 1994), 377. Note the occurrence of the word "lawful" (*exestin*) in both Matt. 14:4 and 19:3.

7. See Heth, "Jesus on Divorce," 11, 16. See also Carson, *Matthew*, 465–66.

8. So rightly Wenham, "Gospel Definitions," 331.

9. See the thorough treatment by David Instone-Brewer, *Divorce and Remarriage in the Bible* (Grand Rapids: Eerdmans, 2002), 189–212.

10. For a thorough discussion of 1 Cor. 7:12–14 see Judith M. Gundry-Volf, "The Least and the Greatest: Children in the New Testament," in *The Child in Christian Thought and Practice*, ed. Marcia Bunge (Grand Rapids: Eerdmans, 2000), 48–53.

11. On the entire section, see the excellent treatment by Gordon D. Fee, *The First Letter to the Corinthians*, New International Commentary on the New Testament (Grand Rapids: Eerdmans, 1987), 290–306. On the phrase "God has called us to peace," see Instone-Brewer, *Divorce and Remarriage in the Bible*, 203.

12. Robert Stein, "Divorce," *Dictionary of Jesus and the Gospels*, ed. Joel B. Green, Scot McKnight, and I. H. Marshall (Downers Grove, IL: InterVarsity, 1992). 194.

13. For a more thorough discussion, see chap. 12 in the 2d edition of *God, Marriage, and Family* (Wheaton, IL: Crossway, 2010).

Chapter 8: God, Marriage, Family and the Church

1. See the helpful survey of the definition of the church in Millard J. Erickson, *Christian Theology* (2d ed.; Grand Rapids: Baker, 1998), 1041–44; 1058–59.

2. See, e.g., Mark Dever, *Nine Marks of a Healthy Church* (Wheaton, IL: Crossway, 2000), "Mark Four: A Biblical Understanding of Conversion" and "Mark Six: A Biblical Understanding of Church Membership."

3. See the discussions in Erickson, *Christian Theology*, 1047–49; Wayne Grudem, *Systematic Theology* (Grand Rapids: Zondervan, 1994), 858–59; and Mark Dever, "The Church," in *A Theology for the Church*, ed. Daniel L. Akin (Nashville: B&H Academic, 2007), 774–75.

4. The following discussion is of necessity suggestive rather than comprehensive. For more thorough treatments see Erickson, *Christian Theology*, 1060–69; Grudem, *Systematic Theology*, 867–69; and Dever, "The Church," 809–15.

GENERAL INDEX

abortion, 80–82, 156
abuse, 160n18
adoption, 93–94, 156; as God's children, 94–95
adultery, 21–22, 47, 50, 51, 9, 136
arsenokoitai (Gk.: "homosexual sin"), 125–26, 127
artificial reproductive technologies (ART), 156;
  artificial insemination (AI), 88–89; biblical
  principles of evaluation, 90–93; gamete
  intrafallopian transfer (GIFT), 89; in vitro
  fertilization (IVF), 89–90; surrogacy, 90
Ash, Christopher, 48, 50, 159nn6–7, 160n14,
  160n17, 160n21, 161n11, 162n26, 165n7
Augustine, 39–40, 162n24

Bailey, D. Sherwin, 119
Barnett, Walter, 119
bᵉrît (Heb.: "covenant"), 44–45
Block, Daniel I., 54, 54–55, 162n18, 163n11, 166n3
Bromiley, Geoffrey, 47
Brown, Peter, 161n1
Bulloch, C. Hassell, 81

celibacy, 49; Jesus's and Paul's teaching on, 106–8,
  110, 157
Chapman, Gary, 41–42
children: in the ministry of Jesus, 67–68; New
  Testament terms for, 64; Old Testament
  fathers' responsibilities toward daughters,
  56; Old Testament fathers' responsibilities
  toward sons, 55–56; Old Testament mothers' responsibilities toward, 57–58; Old
  Testament role and responsibilities of, 58–59;
  Old Testament terms for, 58; in Paul's teaching, 69–71
church, the: as the "body of Christ," 33, 146–47;
  as the "bride of Christ," 148; and family ministry, 151–53; as the "household" or "family
  of God," 147–48; legitimate church membership, 146; as the "new temple," 148; origin of,
  145–46; roles of ("the pillar and foundation
  of the truth"; worship, evangelism, and
  discipling; administration of baptism and the
  Lord's Supper), 148–50; as the "temple of the
  Holy Spirit," 148
"civil union," 46
cohabitation, 112–13
complementarity, 14–15, 38, 98, 117; in ancient
  Israelite marriages, 24–26
continence, 49
contraception, 156; morally impermissible forms
  of contraception (the IUD [intrauterine
  device] and the morning-after pill [RU-486]),
  85; morally permissible forms of contraception (abstinence, the rhythm or calendar
  method, barrier methods), 85; "the pill,"
  86–87; the question of the legitimacy of
  contraception in general, 82–84; sterilization, 85–86
Corinth, 124
Council of Trent (1545–1563), 40

courtship. *See* dating
covenant, 44–45; the new covenant, 44, 45, 109,
  111; the old covenant, 111
creation order, 13–14

Dallas, Joe, 168n14
Danylak, Barry, 108, 109, 110–11, 111
dating, 113
Davies, Bob, 168n14
deō (Gk.: "to bind"), 140
Dever, Mark, 169nn3–4
diathēkē (Gk.: "covenant"), 44
Didache, 81–82
Dillow, Linda, 162n19
discipleship, 28; Jesus's teaching on, 64–67, 68;
  and obedience, 71
discipline, 56, 62, 63–64, 75–76, 95, 156; biblical
  guidelines for, 97–98; the father's primary
  responsibility for, 72–73; New Testament
  term for, 73; physical discipline, 63–64, 73,
  97–98; as the "rod" of correction (book of
  Proverbs), 97
divorce and remarriage, 46, 115–16, 157, 167n21;
  biblical principles for dealing with divorce
  and remarriage, 142–43; and the "exception
  clause," 134–36, 137–38, 139; Jesus's teaching
  on, 29, 133–38; in the Old Testament, 20–21,
  105, 131–32; Paul's teaching on, 138–42
domestication, 14
douloō (Gk.: "to bind"), 140

ekklēsia (Gk.: "church"), 145–46
Erickson, Millard J., 159n3, 169n1, 169nn3–4
'erwat dābār (Heb.: "some indecency," "something
  indecent"), 131–32
'ēšed (Heb.: "covenant"), 44
exposure of newborns, 81–82

fall, the, consequences of, 12, 15–16, 28
family: definition of, 53, 163n1; the nuclear family, 53; roles of (care for the physical, social,
  and spiritual well-being of its members;
  procreation and childrearing; witness to
  Christ), 150–51
family, and Jesus: children in the ministry of
  Jesus, 67–68; Jesus's example, 64; Jesus's
  teaching on the family and discipleship,
  64–67
family, in the Old Testament, 108; the ancient
  Israelite conception of family ("house of a
  father"), 53–54; the importance of teaching
  children about God, 59–64; and patricentrism, 17, 54; the role and responsibilities of
  children, 58–59; the role and responsibilities
  of fathers, 54–56; the role and responsibilities of mothers, 56–58
family, Paul's teachings on: children, 69–71;
  fathers and the importance of fatherhood,
  72–73; "household codes," 69; the importance of older women mentoring younger

170

SCRIPTURE INDEX

Scripture Index

Scripture Index